TO: Angela
       Moreno
From: Leida
        Goulding

God's Blessings
& Love

Thanks for
your Support!!!

Never Limit Yourself!

Let's All Work Together

LINDA PAULDING

NEVER LIMIT YOURSELF!

LET'S ALL WORK TOGETHER

PICKLEBALL

TENNIS

LINDA PAULDING

clfpublishing.org
909.315.3161

Cover design by Senir Design.
Contact info: info@senirdesign.com

ISBN #978-1-945102-94-3

Printed in the United States of America.

Dedications

To my mother and father

Catherine and Aaron Paulding

and

to all the fantastic and fabulous people

around the world whom this book

will touch in whatever manner

Acknowledgments

I acknowledge the following individuals and organization:

My Lord and Savior Jesus, for the journey of this book.

Jeremy Mulford (photographer)
– for creating a beautiful cover photo.

Dr. Cassundra White-Elliott (CLF Publishing, LLC)
- for her outstanding work with publishing this book and making a dream come true.

Dee Henry (Former Director of Tennis and Head Tennis Coach at Biola University)
- a peer who assisted me in becoming a dynamic coach in tennis and pickleball.

Greta
- a friend who would listen to me at any time regarding the completion of this book.

Sis. Kyles
- a praying mentor who helped me to dream the impossible.

Rancho Mirage Public Library
- a wonderful and friendly staff that provided assistance with copying and research information.

Foreword

I have been acquainted with Linda, my friend, for over twelve years. She was teaching tennis in the Los Angeles area to numerous persons, including celebrities and common persons when we met. We met through a fellow missionary person from San Francisco who traveled with us on international outreach trips. About 2018, Linda was introduced to pickleball. She was given an opportunity to coach pickleball in the Palm Springs area and subsequently moved there to pursue her vision.

Linda has been coaching tennis for over twenty years and pickleball for at least four years. The central theme of her book focuses on the pickleball and tennis community working together, which is applicable to any situations where people can work together for the common good in society and everyday life. I'm proud of what this book represents to all people.

Congratulations on this best seller!!

Dr. Bette Stampley

Table of Contents

Introduction

Every person's life consists of seasons, phases through which he/she transitions, traverses, and navigates. Some transitions are desired and expected, while others are undesired, unexpected, and even traumatic. Then, there are some transitions that are apropos (very appropriate to a particular situation or person) even if they are unexpected and filled with tremulous occasions that exist for the sole purpose of shaking one's foundation.

My life has been filled with transitions, some geographical, others educational, and still others career wise. Interestingly, the most significant transition has been in my career. Although it would appear as though the shift was unexpected, it was all part of God's master plan for my life, making it the perfect shift from my status quo to a life of adventure.

The chapters of this book will share the spontaneous transition I was able to experience by "simply" taking a leap of faith. And, believe me, there was nothing "simple" about it. Despite the numerous imbedded challenges I faced, I would not change the experience, for it brought forth abilities that were lying dormant, waiting to rise to the surface to be put into action.

As a result of the transition, I am able to apply the strength and gift of perseverance I had developed in my formative years. I am able to watch God perform miracles as He uses me as an agent of change in the lives of many. I am able to keep my same focus of helping others as I have always desired throughout my lifetime although I changed pathways. I continuously witness God use my inner passion to manifest an outward impact of compassion for those who share like desires.

As I stated, there was nothing simple about my transition. Nevertheless, I am here to share my story for the sole purpose of assisting others in understanding life is not about making singular choices whereby relegating one to maintaining the status quo of his/her life after a decision has been made. As people navigate the various seasons of their life, there needs to be a reassessment of previous choices to see if those decisions (usually made in one's youth) are still viable and fulfilling for the next season.

Having surveyed people over the decades of my life, I have witnessed the majority of people maintaining their status quo because the level of passion they possess is still strong as well as their ability to perform in their career. Conversely, I have come across a segment of the working population who has desired to make changes but neglected to do so due to the belief they were too old or the risks were too high or because they were faced with other issues that prevented them from believing they had viable options they could explore.

I too could have permitted circumstances to freeze me in the position I held and not taken the leap of faith. However, I am overjoyed because I took the leap of faith when I stood at the crossroad and had a choice to make about the direction I would go. One option was to continue on the fruitful and fulfilling path I was on. The other option was to start fully on a new path that would have obstacles but would be just as or more fulfilling as my previous path. I opted for the second choice.

A "Not-So-New" Sport
Pickleball & Me

Swoosh! Swoosh! is all that can be heard along with the taps of the paddle. All the people filling the stands are quiet as their eyes follow the hollow ball as it moves from one side of the court to the other, as the players hit it so craftily. The onlookers do not want to miss a second of the action. The action continues for another ten minutes, with one team serving and then the other.

Suddenly, the ball bounces on the ground, rolls away, and comes to a stop.

A collective gasp can be heard throughout the crowd.

As the match ends, the winning team members lift their paddles in triumph, in victory! Then, a cheer erupts, and the celebration begins as they walk to the net to tap their opponents' paddles.

For many of the onlookers who comprise the audience, it is their first time attending a pickleball tournament. They had just recently heard of the sport, and each time they inquire about it, they are only able to acquire bits and pieces of information along the way.

I must admit when I first heard of pickleball, my curiosity was piqued as well.

It was the Spring of 2018. Yes, just five years ago. I was attending the Southern California Division Convention of the United States Professional Tennis Association (USPTA), held at a country club in Huntington Beach. The primary purpose of the convention was to participate in workshops and sessions over a two-day period to fulfill my annual certification requirement by continuing my education in the field of tennis. There were a variety of speakers over the two days as well as award ceremonies, honoring individuals for their accomplishments.

During the general meeting of the conference, a gentleman was introduced to the attendees, which consisted of tennis coaches from across the state. As I sat in my seat, my eyes followed the man as he approached the podium. I wondered what bit of information he would share with us. After re-introducing himself, he began with a statement that captured and held my attention. "I want to introduce you to a different stream of income. It will be the wave of the future. The game is pickleball," he stated. From the moment he made that statement, I was tuned in.

PICKLE... WHAT?!

When people hear about pickleball, they almost instantly become intrigued and begin to ask questions. Seven of the most often asked questions are:

Question 1- Why has pickleball become so popular at this time even though the sport was invented in 1965 on Bainbridge Island in Seattle, Washington?

Question 2- When will pickleball become exclusively a spectator sport?

Question 3- Is pickleball causing a decline in tennis?

Question 4- Why are tennis courts disappearing?

Question 5- Has the elitism of tennis led to the popularity of pickleball?

Question 6- Which sport will win the battle: tennis or pickleball?

Question 7- Will pickleball become the major racket sport?

And I was just like others, who have loads of questions. After listening to the spiel the man had presented to us, my adrenaline was running high. I wanted to get in on the action, but I wanted to know more about pickleball first. As a result, I did as I had become accustomed to doing when I wanted to know more about something: I researched.

Here is the information I learned:

- According to Onix (2023), pickleball was born in 1965. After playing golf during the summer, Joel Pritchard, a congressman from Washington, and Bill Bell, a successful businessman, returned to Pritchard's home on Bainbridge Island, not far from Seattle, Washington. With bored children at home, they sought to play badminton on an old badminton court but couldn't find the proper equipment. They improvised and played with table tennis paddles and a perforated plastic ball. They began with the net at a badminton net height (60 inches high) and volleyed the ball back and forth over the net. Eventually as play progressed during the weekend, they found the ball bounced well on the asphalt surface and they would eventually lower the net to 36 inches high. The following weekend, Barney McCallum joined and began playing and the three men created the rules for pickleball. The men remembered the original purpose of creating the game was for a game the whole family could play when they were bored.

- By 1967, the first permanent pickleball court was constructed in the backyard of Pritchard's friend and neighbor Bob O'Brian. In 1972, a corporation was formed to protect the sport and in 1975, the National Observer wrote for the first time about pickleball. Tennis magazine followed this with an article about America's newest racquet sport in 1976.

- By spring 1976, the first-known tournament in the world was held at South Center Athletic Club in Tukwila, Washington. Team ONIX's Steve Paranto placed second and David Lester won Men's Singles. Because this was such a new sport and players knew so little about it, at the time of the tournament, they practiced with large wood paddles and a softball-sized whiffle ball.

- In 1978, a book called *The Other Raquet Sports* was published and it included information about pickleball. Four years later, Sid Williams began playing and organizing tournaments in Washington.

- The first pickleball rulebook was published in 1984 by the United States Amateur

Pickleball Association, which committed to growth and advancement of the sport. Sid Williams served as the first executive director and president from 1984 to 1998. Frank Candelario followed him until 2004.

- Steve Paranto's father Arlen Paranto, a Boeing Industrial Engineer, created the first composite pickleball paddle. Arlen used fiberglass and nomex honeycomb panels that the commercial airplanes used for their flooring and structural system. Arlen made 1,000 paddles from this fiberglass/ honeycomb core and graphite/honeycomb core until he sold the company to Frank Candelario.

- By 1990, pickleball was being played in all 50 states. Two years later, Pickle-Ball, Inc. manufactured pickleballs in-house with a custom drilling machine. By 1999, the first ever pickleball website launched called Pickleball Stuff.

- In 2001, pickleball was introduced in the Arizona Senior Olympics drawing 100 players, which was the largest event to be played at that point. Later, events would begin growing to nearly 300 players. By 2003, Pickleball Stuff would list 39 known places to play in North America: 10 states, 3 Canadian Provinces, and 150 individual courts.

- In 2005, the USA Pickleball Association was established. Three years later, the USAPA

Rules Committee published an official rulebook. Pickleball was included for the first time in the National Senior Games Association. *Good Morning America* aired a live segment on pickleball for the first mass media exposure for the sport.

- The first USAPA National Tournament was held in November 2009 and drew almost 400 players from 26 states and several Canadian provinces.
- Since then, pickleball has been exploding in growth and popularity with tournaments played by millions ranging from young to old all over the world. The USAPA has more than 40,000 members and it has estimated pickleball as one of the fastest growing sports in the United States as participants reach around 3.3 million (Onix, 2023).

How did Pickleball get its name?

According to Primetime Pickleball, in a very interesting podcast called The Pickler, guest Roger Belair explains two stories on the possible origins of the name "Pickleball."

The first version of the story is that up until the time the sport got its name, the creators and those around them just referred to it as "the game." But, one day, around 5pm at Pritchard's house (according to Barney McCallum), when the cocktails started flowing, someone in the group suggested they give the game a legitimate name. Some ideas got bounced around such as "rally ball," "tennis pong," etc. Finally, someone pointed out that Pritchard had a dog named Pickle who would always grab the ball and run around with it. Technically, it was "Pickle's Ball." So, it was decided that the game would from then on be called Pickleball (primetimepickleball.com).

(pinterest.com)

The second story that is floating around came about when Joel's ex-wife, Joan, told the media later on in life, 32 years after the game was created, and said that she came up with the name. She said that it came about because of a pickle boat and the dog actually came later on. What is a pickle boat you may be asking yourself? A pickle boat is when you take different parts of different boats and put them together to create a new boat.

Now there exist these two different stories that are quite the topic of conversation in the pickleball community. According to Primetime Pickleball, Roger BelAir says he tends to believe that whatever story people hear first is usually the one they think is the right one.

Barney McCallum, Joel Pritchard, and Bill Bell

After a bit more research, I found the following information on the name of the game:

"In the summer of 1965, pickleball was founded by Joel Pritchard, Bill Bell and Barney McCallum on Bainbridge Island, Washington. Within days, Joan Pritchard had come up with the name "pickle ball"—a reference to the thrown-together leftover non-starters in the "pickle boat" of crew races. Many years later, as the sport grew, a controversy ensued when a few neighbors said they were there when Joan named the game after the family dog, Pickles. Joan and the Pritchard family have held fast for decades that the dog came along a few years later and was named after the game. It's an undisputed fact that pickleball began, and was also named, in the summer of 1965 by Joan Pritchard. If Pickles was around then, the dog story could be true. If Pickles wasn't born until after 1965, the dog story would be confirmed as just a funny newspaper interview hoax— later confessed by Joel Pritchard. Proof of when Pickles was born could help resolve the two-story name debate. As the official magazine of pickleball, we decided to dig up the past and report the truth, regardless of the venerable feathers being ruffled. We looked for dog records, uncovered photos, and interviewed several people who were there from 1965-1970. Based on evidence, we learned that the dog was born in 1968— three years after pickleball was first played and named. In other words, the Pritchard family story stands true that pickleball was not named after the dog, but rather in reference to the local pickle boat races" (USA Pickleball, 2023).

After learning about pickleball at the tennis conference (while in the midst of researching its history), I began to earnestly search for a place to learn how to play the game. After much effort and finding out that pickleball courts were few and far in between in my local area, I was finally able to locate one in Norwalk, the Norwalk Art & Sports Complex. Having that location as a gem raised my excitement exponentially, and I practiced as often as I could. It has always been my position that if I am going to coach others in a specific skill set, then I should be the best player I can be while being extremely knowledgeable in that skill set as well.

About a month later, after learning the game by playing approximately two days a week, I introduced pickleball in La Mirada, where I was actively coaching tennis. A few of my tennis students along with several others comprised a group of 15-20 older business men who took a liking to pickleball. Together, we practiced the game on Saturdays in the late afternoon. While I was excited about the opportunity to play and develop my skills, several onlookers who watched found our engagement rather curious and basically ludicrous and hilarious. They would snicker and whisper about what we were doing. Frankly, they found our activity odd. They probably thought it was something we had made up.

Little did they know, pickleball was a recognized sport, one that upon its inception had targeted older adults ranging from 50-70 years of age combining three popular games together. According to Primetime Pickleball, "tennis, badminton, and ping pong (table tennis). It is played on a badminton sized court with an approximate tennis height net ([two] inches lower) and what can be thought of as an enlarged ping pong paddle. The pickleball itself is a wiffle ball." The sets are played for fifteen to twenty-five minutes compared to a tennis match, which is approximately ninety minutes for the winner to gain the best of three sets.

Despite the initial reaction of onlookers and the slow growth of pickleball in its early years, much has occurred in the world of pickleball from its inception in 1965 to present day, with the most growth occurring in the last two to three years- during and after the COVID-19 pandemic. The following facts and projections indicate the future of pickleball and the speed of its newfound popularity.

- According to Geeter (2022), pickleball is the fastest-growing sport in America, with over 4.8 million people playing the game. However, its rapid growth has caused some growing pains, stemming from competing professional leagues, managing hundreds of tournaments, a lack of courts to meet demand and channeling the flood of investments.
- By 2030, pickleball is projected to attract an estimated 40 million players across the

globe, with even more investors jumping in looking to cash in on the craze.

- Pickleball has existed since 1965, but it wasn't until people were looking for a participatory sport during the pandemic that its popularity soared. From 2016 to 2019, pickleball grew an average of 7.2% annually in the U.S. from 2.8 million players to 3.5 million, but that growth skyrocketed 39.3% from 2020 to 2021, with 4.8 million Americans playing the racket sport. And over the past five years, pickleball saw an average annual growth of 11.5%, while similar sports like badminton and pingpong saw negative growth of -3.7% and -1.2%, respectively. What's more, pickleball is being played by people across a broad spectrum of age and income levels, according to a 2021 report by the Sports & Fitness Industry Assc.

- That surging popularity has led to a spate of team investments and growing equipment sales, with the pickleball paddle market size expected to grow 68% from $152.8 million in 2021 to a forecasted $256.1 million by 2028, according to Absolute Reports.

- Professional leagues are competing for players, with Major League Pickleball, or MLP, which just launched last year, making headlines with investments in the seven-figure range from celebrity athletes like LeBron James and Tom Brady. Next year, the

MLP is looking to expand from 12 teams to 16 and to shell out over $2 million in prize money.

LeBron James   Tom Brady

- While the United States is seen as the mecca of pickleball, advocates are hoping it will get a worldwide forum if it were to be introduced as a sport at the 2028 Summer Olympics games in Los Angeles.
- One potential downside has come with the pickleball craze. In recent years, the tournament scene has exploded with a deluge of events, as organizers attempt to keep up with the demand. In consequence, player health and safety has become a growing concern for some players and event organizers.
- "The sport is changing. It's getting physically and grueling, and it's a lot on our bodies," Kyle Yates, a professional pickleball player and tournament organizer, told CNBC. "I know that a lot of tournaments are run in a way where the players really aren't the first priority, and they should be. And so there's a lot of new players coming in that are training

and playing a lot of tournaments, and physically it might be too much to them."

- From its humble beginnings as a simple pickup game for the family to enjoy to significant investment opportunities, with an estimated 40 million players by 2030, pickleball's gold rush isn't ending anytime soon (Geeter, 2022).

After I learned about pickleball in 2018, my participation in the sport developed at a rapid pace. By 2019, after having been involved in the sport for less than a year, I began coaching on a regular basis, while still actively coaching tennis. The growth of the sport was intriguing to me, but what also caught my attention was the fact that similar to many other instances in my life, I was one of the first few persons of color (if not the first) who engaged in coaching and playing in tournaments in the Palms Springs area. While that was intriguing, I knew there would be an evolution of involvement over time. I just had no idea it would happen sooner than I could have imagined.

Times magazine concurs with other researchers that pickleball is the fastest-growing sport in America, according to the Sports & Fitness Industry Association (SFIA). And [Paul] Rivera, along with a coterie of NBA stars, like [LeBron] James, [Draymond] Green, and [Kevin] Love, want in. On Sept. 28, Major League Pickleball (MLP), the fledgling pro league, announced that is received a seven-figure investment from a group, headlined by James, to purchase a new team. The investors includes LRMR Ventures, the family office of [LeBron] James and [Maverick] Carter; Green; Love; Rivera; investment firm SC Holdings; and Daniel Sillman, co-owner and CEO of Relevent Sports Group, a media and promotion company. Major League Pickleball already receives some mainstream media coverage—CBS Sports Network has telecast the finals of MLP events—and since the announcement of James' involvement, MLP strategic advisor Anne Worcester says the league has received more than 100 inquiries from interested owners and sponsors, as the league expands from 12 to 16 teams, from three to six events, and from $1 million to $2 million in prize money next year. Ironically, the investments made by athletes occurred after Serena Williams retired.

"This group brings us unparalleled experience across sports, across media, across branding and entertainment," says Worcester. "Plus, the celebrity angle just expands the reach of the sport immensely. It's a major moment for the sport of pickleball." I noticed an intense rise in the popularity of the sport after these well-known, affluent athletes demon-strated their interest in the sport. After basketball legends, such as Lebron James, Draymond Green, and Kevin Durant, and football stars, such as Tom Brady became involved (along with other male millionaires and billionaires who have invested in pickleball), their involvement has taken pickleball to a different level. Furthermore, there was an influx of young people who became interested in learning the game.

There are currently some 5 million pickleball players in the U.S., according to SFIA data; partici-pation jumped 39.3% from 2019 to 2021. Some 40% of pickleball players are under 35, according to SFIA. "Gone are the days of 'pickleball's for seniors,'" says Worcester.

MLP has set a goal for the sport to reach 40 million players by 2030. Pickleball became popular among NBA referees, team personnel, and media members looking to kill time in the NBA's 2020 COVID-19 bubble in Orlando: as a non-contact sport played outdoors, the risks of catching the virus while playing seemed low. Rivera, a former Nike exec, says that James, Love, and

Green are all fans of the sport. Like many others, Rivera himself started playing pickleball during the pandemic, initially on a work trip with Carter in Mexico in 2020.

In early 2019, I had begun traveling from Los Angeles (where I resided and coached tennis) to the Palm Springs area, in the Coachella Valley, two to three days per week to coach pickleball. By the summer months, my increasing pickleball schedule led me to have residences in both areas to reduce the wear and tear on my body and vehicle from driving the miles each day and night. By the time 2019 was coming to a close, I finally resolved to relinquishing my Los Angeles' residence in exchange for residing in the Palm Springs area. My schedule had greatly shifted, and pickleball had begun to consume most of my time. It was an exhilarating time for me. I was on the cusp of something great, and I was ready for it! I had always believed everything has its due season, and I knew within the depths of my spirit the season for pickleball had arrived. From that moment, I planned to ride the waves with it.

My exposure to the game and to those who had a growing zeal for it led to many doors of opportunity opening for me as well as personal growth. In November 2019, I was certified as a professional pickleball coach. From there, I continued building my clientele as well as my own skills by engaging in round-robin practice tournaments. These are tournaments were players of all skill levels can join in to play and increase their skill level with the understanding that these tournaments are just for fun.

However, many of the naysayers held fast to their mindset saying, "It's not going anywhere. It will be just like racket ball." Ignoring their disbelief, I held fast to what the Lord was showing me. Like other moments in my life, I held fast to my faith, believing if God brought me to it, He would definitely see me through it.

My skill development led me to compete in tournaments, which was exciting, yet sometimes nerve wracking at the beginning, as I was getting my feet wet and becoming grounded. The first conference I had the pleasure of competing in was the Desert Pickleball Classic, held in Palm Desert, CA in 2020. For me, the tournament was tedious because I had no idea what I was doing as it related to policies and procedures. Lacking that necessary information, I had a difficult time during the tournament, making errors I could have avoided if I had been abreast of the minute details. To compound matters, I was extremely nervous because in my quest to learn pickleball and enter the competitive circuit, I began playing at a high level with skilled players. Their ability on the court and knowledge of the game was intimidating to say the least.

Overall, I was able to handle my own, while finding the tournament exhilarating. Surprisingly, despite the feelings that were quite overwhelming at the beginning, I secured a medal! I was able to leave the tournament being very proud of myself despite beginning the match prior to the referee giving the official start command. Mentally, I vowed to never allow that to happen again. It was a learning experience, and I definitely knew more at the end of the tournament than I did at the beginning. I guess you could consider it on-the-job training so to speak.

The next year, in June 2021, I decided to enter the USAPA Pickleball National Indoor Championship to continue becoming familiar with pickleball tournaments in general and to get my name out there. That tournament held an additional layer of excitement for me as it was taking place in Hoover, Alabama, which was near my hometown of Bessemer, Alabama. I entered the tournament with increased comfort and confidence levels than I had during the Desert Pickleball Classic the year prior. At that point in my pickleball career, I had another year of practicing under my belt and had strengthened my personal game and skill level. The tournament lasted for approximately one week with over 2,000 participants. Although I felt more comfortable with the game, the matches were still very challenging, keeping me alert as I swung my paddle high and low.

Because the tournament was held in Alabama where I was raised, I was able to have more support during the tournament when family members, friends, and former tennis comrades joined the audience of spectators. They were happy to see me back in Alabama during that timeframe, and everyone was excited I was involved in this "new" sport. One person in particular who I was able to reconnect with was Mr. Rudy Lewis. He and I had played tennis together in Birmingham at Ensley Park years earlier. During the pickleball tournament, he was a referee. He served as the first president of the James Lewis Tennis Foundation.

As I interacted with friends and family while in Alabama, some laughed and joked with me saying, "Only you, Lynn. Of course, *you* would play." I laughed along with them because they had me pegged correctly. I was certainly willing to give the game a try. Others had questions because prior to the tournament coming to Alabama, they had never heard of pickleball. Just as the average person had been asking, some of my family and friends inquired (with Question 6): "Is pickleball going to replace or overtake or cause tennis to become obsolete?"

At the validity, yet absurdity, of the question, I shook my head and responded with what had become my typical response: "Neither will win. There is room for both sports. Both sports can continue to thrive. Think of it this way. There are many hamburger places where a person can choose to eat. Look at how In-N-Out Burger has grown in popularity. When you drive by a local franchise, you may see a line of cars heading for the drive-thru window. But despite In-N-Out's growing popularity, the other hamburger joints, such as McDonald's, Burger King, and Carl's Jr., have not gone out of business. There is room for all of them to thrive. So, when it comes to tennis and pickleball, there is room for both of them to thrive. It does not have to be one or the other."

If that example did not assist in their understanding that two sports can coexist at one time, I often provided this one: "With the increase in the use of email for an effective means of communication, the post office has still not gone out of business. Some people not only mail packages, but they still mail letters." When I provided those explanations and examples, I saw heads nod up and down in understanding. When I consider the disgruntlement occurring between tennis and pickleball, I mentally ask myself, "Why can't players of the two sports get along?" Then, I say to myself, "I believe I am here to bridge the gap between the two."

Proponents of both tennis and pickleball
(American Tennis Association (ATA) Event)

Near the end of 2021, in the month of September, I participated in my third tournament, which was the West Regional Fountain Valley Tournament in California. I engaged confidently with the other participants that numbered in excess of 2,000. Over a span of four days, I played singles (one on one) and mixed doubles (both sexes, two on two) in various divisions with opponents of varying skill levels. Although the tournament was very strenuous, I won a medal. I felt more comfortable than I had been in Alabama that summer and in Palm Desert the year before. I also felt an increased level of excitement I had not experienced before because my discomfort and anxiety had not left much room for contentment. Furthermore, I knew my participation (and the wins) in that tournament along with the previous one would qualify me to participate in the National tournament: the Margaritaville USAPA National Championship two months later in Indian Wells, CA.

Going to Nationals had been my dream for the short time I had been engaged in pickleball. Just thinking about it caused exhilaration about the possibility to rise within me. The first time Margaritaville had been held was in 2018, and it had grown in popularity in a matter of two to three years. That tournament was on such a grand scale that players could not simply sign up for it. Rather, players had to qualify by participating and placing in other tournaments prior to submitting an application. My participation in the USAPA National Indoor Championship and the West Regionals had qualified me for Margaritaville. But, simply qualifying and having the experience of the other three tournaments did not mean I was not nervous about participating in a national tournament where players from all over the United States and other parts of the world would come to play.

Before any tournament, whether it was a regional one that included local players or a national one, it is always a good idea to have proper mental, physical, and emotional rest prior to the matches. Having been an avid tennis player and coach, I was very familiar with that routine behavior, as I had adopted it many years before. But on the nights leading up to the convention as well as all the nights of the convention, I did not sleep well at all. Nervousness filled my stomach, debilitating my sleep pattern. While lying awake, I imagined myself playing against a variety of players who possessed skill sets superior to mine. My mind went from one thought to the next as I imagined one scenario then another. I truly did not know what to expect.

Despite the mental anguish I experienced during the nights, each day that I showed up for the tournament, I went in with my game face and gave each match my all. I could not really do less than that, could I? No, of course not. That is not at all how I operate. I have never given anything I have done half my effort. If I am going to do something, I am going to put everything I have into it. The National Tournament would be no different. All in all, I had the time of my life! I was nervous, but I did not allow the nerves to impede my progress. The matches were very challenging, but I hung in there as I played singles and mixed doubles, and I did very well. All the practicing I had done from 2018 up to that point paid off. I was able to hold my own. Although I did not take any medals home, it was an opportunity of a lifetime, and I am pleased to have had it. Like all the other tournaments, it was an experience I will never forget.

The next year, in the Spring of 2022, I had an opportunity to participate in additional tournaments that would be held during the summer months. However, as I continued to assimilate into the Palms Springs' culture, I learned more about the behaviors of the locals. Due to the extremely arid climate and the heat waves of the Greater Palm Springs area during the summer months, many residents and coaches departed the three degree, sweltering temperatures, opting for cooler climates. Some of the coaches left for places such as Wisconsin and Colorado to train clients, and others went elsewhere to relax, hone their own skills, or take up golf in their free time. In March, I learned of coaching opportunities in the Hamptons, a location on my list of travel destinations. Knowing the weather would be much more pleasant in the Hamptons, I opted to travel there to coach and escape the scorching heat of Palm Springs.

Once I had discussed employment with the West Hampton Tennis and Sport in the Hamptons (Bobby) and had reached an agreement regarding coaching pickleball there in June, my excitement increased continuously, not only about traveling to a much-desired location, but because of pickleball's growing popularity. Once my travel arrangements were set, I then had to secure a place of lodging for the duration of my stay. Speaking with my soon-to-be employer, I was told the Hamptons were always very busy in the summer months and locating a place to lodge would prove difficult, but they would do what they could to assist me. Thankfully, they were true to their word.

Prior to my arrival, I had no idea what to expect regarding the condition of the courts, the skill level of the players, or much of anything, as I had never been to the Hamptons before. Regardless of the lack of my working knowledge, I was tremendously excited about the prospect of surrounding myself with another group of people who were excited to learn the game of pickleball, and the country club staff was equally as excited regarding my impending arrival. I could hear the excitement in their voices when they said, "We would love to have you in June."

When June arrived, I exited the plane in New York and took a train into the Hamptons, making my way to the country club. When I had an opportunity to check out the courts, not surprisingly, there were more tennis courts than pickleball courts. As a matter of fact, they had just begun the conversion of some of the tennis courts over to pickleball courts the month prior. And, as I had seen on many previous occasions, the tennis courts had been restriped and converted into pickleball courts. Those conversions were common-place from city to city and state to state. Unfortunately, the conversions had led to many lawsuits. The facilities (country clubs, sporting facilities, etc.) who were responsible for allowing the tennis courts to be restriped were unwilling to fully convert the courts over or use available space to have pickleball courts constructed due to the "newness" of the game. They did not want to risk the financial investment.

From their perspective, pickleball was off to a slow start, just as tennis had been in the 70s and 80s. People, despite their growing interest in the sport, did not want to get ahead of themselves by having expectations that could easily falter. They were content with waiting it out. They were wise in their thinking; however, I cannot say I was in agreement with their train of thought. From what I had seen from 2018 to that point, I knew that regardless of the small amounts of money available a few years earlier, increased revenues had begun to filter into the sport.

When I first began learning and coaching pickleball, there was not a lot of money to be made as a professional player. However, with the rapid growth over the last few years, the statistics have changed. Tournament participants can earn anywhere from $20-30k. With the tremendous growth pickleball has experienced, I fully expect to see the first pickleball millionaire in the next few years, if not sooner.

Even the number of pickleball sponsors has increased. Personally, Babolat (Allan) (a major tennis and pickleball brand) has been my sponsor for clothing and paddles for pickleball. They have been very supportive of my career, and I appreciate their generosity.

Regardless of the condition of the courts in the Hamptons, the players were excited to learn the game, and I exuded an equal amount of energy, displaying my excitement about the opportunity to engage with them as they learned the rules. The clientele there ranged from the affluent to Wall Street business executives to housewives to celebrities, who were all looking for a fun hobby that was not too strenuous or taxing on the body.

For me, working with celebrities was exciting, but it was nothing new. I had worked with a number of them throughout my career, coaching some in tennis, others in pickleball, and some in both. Many of my previous sessions with the celebs had taken place in their homes, which were located in the Greater Los Angeles area, from Beverly Hills, to Bel Air, to Hollywood, to Malibu. By that time, I had come to be known as the celebrity tennis and pickleball coach.

Just as it had been with the celebs in California, my clients in the Hamptons were fun to work with. While I learned their ways of life when visiting their beautiful homes (many of which were on the beach), they learned to stop referring to the paddle as a racket. I was able to offer many training lessons at the club; however, I offered private and group lessons as well for both pickleball and tennis. To my delight, many people who had never engaged in a sport before had taken a liking to pickleball. In particular, many women were thrilled about the game, and their husbands were delightedly surprised about their engagement because they had never demonstrated their athleticism.

While engaging with the Hampton's unique clientele, I began to view pickleball as somewhat of an academic sport. The game includes many unique rules that are very detailed, causing it to be mentally challenging, similar to the game of chess. Pickleball quickly captured the attention of those who always had a desire to play a sport but lacked a specific skill set to do well. That is not to say skilled athletes cannot or should not play. The game is for all people: those with honed skills and those who have never engaged in a sport before. Interestingly, pickleball originally attracted mostly mature adults due to its low impact, but now it has attracted people of all ages, from all skill levels. As a result, the non-pro tour pickleball tournaments include all levels of players, from recreational players (amateurs) to professionals, allowing for 2-3,000 participants playing in a tournament while the professional tour allows for approximately 75 men and 75 women to participate. A tennis tournament, on the other hand, usually includes approximately 150-200 professional men and women players, in their respective tours.

In December 2022, I became employed by the J. W. Marriott (which is also inclusive of the Ritz Carlton), as a pickleball coach. (More details are shared in the tennis chapter.) And, I am looking forward to teaching in Martha's Vineyard in the near future.

With pickleball's accelerated growth, it has piqued the curiosity of many people around the country, and the following question (#1) is often asked: "Why has pickleball become so popular at this time even though the sport was invented in 1965 on Bainbridge Island in Seattle, Washington?" I was curious about the perspective of others who are involved in the sport, so I repeated the question to a Bainbridge Island pickleball group leader, and he stated, "That sport is popular because of its great inclusivity of people, such as both youth and mature individuals. Men and women can play each other and have a great fun time." Furthermore, he stated, "The sport is very social."

I agree with his statements; however, I have a few additional thoughts about why pickleball is very popular today. First, pickleball primarily gained its popularity with mature people who wanted to continue playing a sport such as tennis, but it became challenging. Most people in the sport play doubles, and the court coverage is small compared to other sports such as tennis. Second, there is a shortened learning curve, meaning there are not as many rules involved in the game. Third, the games and sets are shorter, leaving less room for fatigue. Fourth, it is a fun sport and very social. Fifth, the overhead serve is not included in this sport. Most players are grateful for that because to execute the overhead serve, a player must be able to toss consistently and must have the strength and coordination to hit the ball over the net using an overhand throwing motion.

Another reason for the sport's popularity is the fact that the wiffle ball is very light as it is made of plastic and has holes in it, causing it to be only an outer shell with a hollow interior. The lightweight ball is easy to handle and hit. Additionally, the players are generally friendly, making it easy to find others to play socially. And, mature people introduced the sport to their children and grandchildren. Further, the tournaments offer amateurs of all levels and ages an opportunity to play alongside professional players. Usually, there are many more amateurs than professional players.

Another contribution to pickleball's accelerated growth in addition to popular athletes being involved in the sport is the involvement of other well-known individuals and celebrities. For example, Bill Gates, philanthropist and co-founder of Microsoft, can be seen demonstrating and introducing pickleball on YouTube; thereby, sparking people's interest. Unbeknownst to many, "Gates grew up near the birthplace of pickleball. He and his family were some of the first people to ever play the game. His dad, Bill Gates, Sr. was friends with the inventors: Joel Pritchard, Barney McCallum, and Bill Bell. Shortly after playing at the original court, Gates' father had a court installed at their home. Gates grew up playing the game and now has been playing for over 50 years" (The Dink Media Team, 2022).

(The Dink Media Team, 2022)

Tiger Woods has made statements on television; Kardashians can be seen playing pickleball on at least one of the episodes of *Keeping Up with the Kardashians*. Jamie Foxx has reportedly been seen in the Palm Springs area playing pickleball. Emmy Award-winner Stephen Colbert of THE LATE SHOW hosts the new two-hour sports comedy special PICKLED, where eight celebrity teams compete in a cutthroat pickleball competition, vying for bragging rights and to benefit Comic Relief. Throughout various media platforms, including the Morning Show, statements regarding pickleball are being made as more and more people learn about the sport.

Because pickleball is closely related to tennis due to the various similarities between the two, they are often compared with one another. The comparison leads to a discussion about the state of tennis, causing many concerns to surface. One of the foremost questions that is asked is Question 4: "Is pickleball causing a decline in tennis?" Why is this question asked so frequently? Well, pickleball has taken tennis real estate at a great pace in the past three to four years, demonstrating both a growing interest in pickleball and a declining interest in tennis, which explains why tennis courts are disappearing. The commandeering of tennis courts demonstrates pickleball's uprising. For example, pickleball has become quite popular in New York. As a result, pickleball courts have been built in Central Park.

(cbsnews.com)

Question 5 is becoming more and more common: Has the elitism of tennis led to the popularity of pickleball? Lawn tennis started in England on grass with the king and queen in attendance, especially at the major Grand Slam, Wimbledon. Some people regarded it as a royalty sport. When I grew up in Alabama playing tennis, we always watched Wimbledon yearly. Many tennis players like myself dreamt of playing in that prestigious tournament.

The following statistics further illustrate pickleball's growth and increasing popularity.

Key Pickleball Stats for 2023

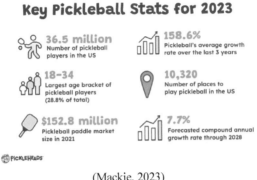

(Mackie, 2023)

- There are currently 36.5 million pickleball players estimated in the United States according to the Association of Pickleball Professionals in 2022.
- Pickleball participation has grown an average of 158.6% over the last 3 years according to the SFIA.
- Pickleball is the fastest-growing sport in America for the past three years.
- Players 18-34 make up the largest percentage of pickleball players at 28.8% nationwide.
- There are currently 10,320 pickleball courts in the United States.
- The pickleball paddle market size is estimated at $152.8 million in 2021 and is forecasted to grow at 7.7% CAGR through 2028.
(Mackie, 2023)

This exponential growth may move pickleball to become the major racket sport over tennis (Question 6) and cause it to become exclusively a spectator sport, which I anticipate occurring in approximately three to five years (Question 2).

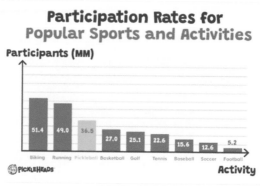

(Mackie, 2023)

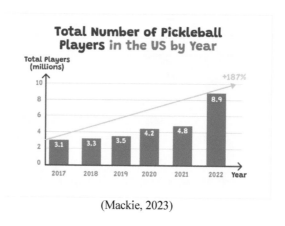

(Mackie, 2023)

Year	Total Pickleball Players
2017	3,132,000
2018	3,301,000
2019	3,460,000
2020	4,200,000
2021	4,820,000
2022	8,900,000

(Mackie, 2023)

- According to the Sports & Fitness Industry Association (SFIA), more than 8.9 million people play pickleball across the US in 2022 (over the age of 6).
- That's nearly double (85.7%) the 4.8 million players reported in the United States the previous year, and a whopping 158.6% increase over the past 3 years! (Mackie, 2023)

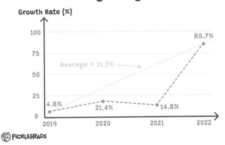

(Mackie, 2023)

Year	Annual Pickleball Growth Rate %
2017	11.3%
2018	5.4%
2019	4.8%
2020	21.4%
2021	14.8%
2022	85.7%

(Mackie, 2023)

Pickleball Players by Gender

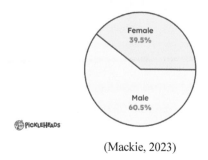

(Mackie, 2023)

- Women grew slightly faster than men, at 17.6% year-over-year in 2021, compared to men who grew at 13.0% year-over-year.
- Pickleball Demographics: Players by Age
- Players aged 55 and up were the largest age bracket of pickleball players in 2021, comprising 19.8% of total participants. Players aged 18 to 34 were the second largest age bracket, making up 18.5% of total participants.
- The average age of pickleball players was 38.1 years in 2021. The average age of pickleball players is dropping and declined 2.9 years from an average of 41.0 years in 2020.
- Pickleball player growth in 2021 was the fastest among players under 24 years of age (21%). Growth among players 55 and older was slower at 10% year-over-year.
- There will be 47 major pickleball tournaments held in the US across 2023 between the top three pro tours: Major League Pickleball (MLP), The Professional Pickleball Association (PPA) and the

American Association of Pickleball Professionals (APP).

- The total prize pool of pickleball tournaments to be held in 2023 will be between $9.0 and $11.0 million. (Mackie, 2023)

Pickleball Tournament Stats

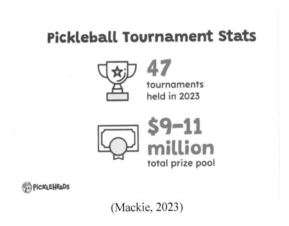

47 tournaments held in 2023

$9–11 million total prize pool

PICKLEHEADS

(Mackie, 2023)

    I had an opportunity to interview Roger BelAir, and this is the information he provided:
He has upcoming trips in May 2023 planned for prison facilities, such as San Quentin, Folsom, CA State, and State Medical Facility to teach pickleball. Regarding the growth of pickleball, he stated when baby boomers retired in 2002/2003, the growth of pickleball began during 2017/2018, and admist the pandemic, the growth really developed, especially regarding media attention and celebrities in the past several years. He confirmed Pritchard's dog was named Pickles and that's from where the game was named because the dog would run after the ball. Also, he stated prior to that name, pickleball was called

"The Game." He stated pickleball is such a fun sport and not necessarily a spectator sport. Also, he was well acquainted with Barney McCallum (original founder) prior to his departure.

An article in the Washington Post about Roger BelAir shares the following:

Pickleball's latest court? The prison yard.
It's conquered local parks and cable television. Now, with the help of one obsessed player, one of America's fastest-growing sports is spreading to state prisons.

BUSHNELL, Fla. — Paddle in hand, Roger BelAir shifted side to side as he was introduced to that day's audience. He was eager to get started, to tell everyone about the game he felt could change their lives.
"Everyone know the rules?" he asked.
"Well, I believe in following the rules, so let's talk about that today."
The prison was slowly coming to life, and BelAir could feel the morning temperature climbing. The closest he'd ever come to breaking the law: minor parking violations back home near Seattle. But this game, he was convinced, is a force of good, bridging gaps and offering life lessons. So here he was at the Sumter Correctional Institution, about 50 miles north of Tampa, talking to a couple dozen inmates about pickleball.
It was Day 7 of BelAir's eight-day trek across Florida. Each day brought him into a new prison, with a new group of felons and a new chance to introduce a sport that has already gripped much of the population outside.

The Sumter prison yard is encased by barbed wire. Guard towers loom, corrections officers are ever-present. This group of prisoners had earned perks through good behavior, which on this day put them in front of BelAir, 76, who crisscrosses the country on his own dime and volunteers his time behind bars because he thinks pickleball has some answers these inmates need, a skeleton key of sorts to rehabilitation.

"Something like 95 percent of people are eventually released from prison," he says. "If we can make them better people on the inside, it's better for all of us once they get back outside."

BelAir eagerly explained the game. It's a cross between tennis, table tennis and badminton, he told them. It was invented in 1965 on Bainbridge Island, Wash., and is now the fastest-growing sport in the country. He told them pickleball had a way of breaking down barriers and is accessible to players of all ages and backgrounds.

That resonated with the prisoners, a group surrounded by barriers. Everyone here wears a similar ID badge and prison-issued T-shirt and light blue shorts, but their backgrounds, criminal charges and prison sentences vary wildly. The inmates that circled the pickleball court included convicted murderers, sex offenders, drug dealers. Some would be out in a couple of years; others would never leave.

BelAir is convinced the sport could benefit them all, and it wasn't long before the inmates started to understand why. After he demonstrated how to serve, the prisoners spread across two courts and began tapping the ball back and forth over the net. There was laughter, encouragement, some gentle ribbing.

"For a bit, it really takes your mind away from being in prison," one inmate said.

That's part of BelAir's grander vision. He wants to make the game a staple of prison life. Not just in Florida, but everywhere. And he's taking it upon himself to spread the pickle gospel.

BelAir didn't tell the prisoners his own backstory — how he'd found success in banking and investing, discovered pickleball late in life and, at 64, was instantly hooked. How he took up coaching and staged clinics and slowly started building his life around the sport.

Instead, BelAir told them about a night five years ago that he and his wife were watching an episode of "60 Minutes" that featured a segment on Tom Dart, the sheriff of Cook County, Ill., who oversees one of the largest jails in the country. BelAir was struck by footage of inmates standing idle and had an idea.

"I said to my wife, 'They ought to be playing pickleball,'" BelAir recalled. "They'd get exercise, learn life lessons — sportsmanship, learning from mistakes — so I tell my wife, 'I'm gonna write him a letter. And I'll go out there and I'll teach them all pickleball.'

"My wife, of course, gave me the ol' eye-roll," he said.

But he did. Dart recalls receiving BelAir's letter not long after. He didn't know what pickleball was, but he shared the proposal with his staff. The sheriff was intrigued.

"He was offering something for free, which obviously got my attention in a hurry," Dart says.

He did some research, made sure the equipment wasn't likely to be used as a weapon and opened the jail doors to BelAir.

"It was full steam ahead," Dart says. "He was very passionate about this. And there were no strings attached, which in my world is very rare. You just have this sort of altruistic person who just wants to do this."

BelAir flew to Chicago and brought the game with him. Soon there were more letters and more prison visits. He went to Rikers Island in New York, Corcoran in California, and facilities in New Hampshire, Alaska and Washington state.

Covid slowed his efforts, but as restrictions began to subside, he was eager to get back on the road. Last year, he pitched Florida, where Department of Corrections officials considered his unique proposal. It's not often someone offers to travel across the country on his own dime, hoping to interact with as many prisoners as possible.

From their perspective, the offer touched on a core tenant of the department's philosophy, engaging inmates, reducing idleness and giving them purpose. Patrick Mahoney, the department's director of Programs and Re-Entry, said inmate wellness "can be a predictive activity for recidivism."

"So if we make a positive impact on somebody's health and wellness, we have made an impact on the potential of reducing recidivism within our agency," he said. "We know the importance of sports. It's a structured way to teach people healthy competition, teach them how to work in groups, how to work together, teamwork. Just like in regular society, it works very well in a prison setting."

While BelAir was introducing pickleball to many inmates for the first time, the game isn't new in all of Florida's prisons. At Sumter, the inmates assembled their own net and started playing a hybrid game on an old tennis court a few years back. They started with a racquetball, but whenever the ball touched barbed wire fencing, an alarm sounded and privileges were revoked. Volunteers eventually donated proper pickleball equipment, and a handful of players are out there every day now, even organizing occasional tournaments.

At the Lowell Correctional Institution, an all-women's facility outside of Ocala, they've been playing for a couple of years. The inmates laid a cement slab over a grassy area and built their own courts. Every Wednesday, a local volunteer comes in to provide instruction.

"I found it was a great way to lose weight, it wasn't hard on your joints. So we just started playing a lot and really fell in love with it," said Sara Denn, 43, who's serving time for drug-related offenses and credit card fraud.

The inmates have recreation time in the yard twice a day. They walk laps, do aerobics or mill around picnic tables. But the pickleball courts have become a respite for a handful of them. "It takes you out of the gates, you know," said Jenise Ortiz, 40.

The prisoners say it's both a distraction from prison life and something that connects them to the outside world. For many, it's a glimpse of what their lives might be like when they're released.

"A lot of times we hear about what we can't do when we get out. We're felons, maybe we have this stigma," said Jolene Elkin, 53, who's serving a life sentence for murder. "With pickleball, there's no stigma. It's all positive. Maybe we don't have opportunities in other areas, but this is something we can try to excel at."

Leslee Pippin, the warden who oversees some 2,000 prisoners at the Lowell lockup, says there have been no drawbacks: Pickleball hasn't sparked fights or created divisions.

"When people are idle, they get bored," Pippin said. "That's when people get argumentative, they start looking for ways to break rules. When they have something positive to do, it keeps them out of trouble. And if there's the temptation of doing something wrong, the thought of losing something like this serves as a deterrent."

The Lowell inmates pass the day reliving points from their morning games and anticipating afternoon rematches. Many say they intend to continue playing the game long after their prison days are over. Ortiz has been locked up since she was 17, when she was convicted of second-degree murder and arson. She's now 40 and has six years remaining on her sentence.

"I wish I had something like this when I was younger," she said. "I was a kid of an incarcerated parent, and I know if we can get kids of incarcerated parents to be interested in something, they can unleash their frustrations and hurts. Introducing a new game to the inner city kids would give me an opportunity to mentor, something that would help them."

For this group, BelAir talked a bit more about technique and strategy before sending them off to play games. "Any questions?" he asked first.

"When are you coming back?" one inmate asked.

There is no research on pickleball's effect on an inmate population, but BelAir notices the impact in every facility he walks into. In Chicago, pickleball is now a staple of the Cook County jail.

"Just like myself, we have to explain to people what it is at first," Dart says, "but it has been wildly popular."

BelAir was encouraged by what he saw as he journeyed across Florida, driving his rental car to prisons from Tallahassee to Orlando.

"This game I'm sure is great for the outside world. But it is something that's very needed in here," said 34-year-old Jhoan Cadavid, a convicted murderer and new pickleball convert.

The facility is like a mini-city with a chapel, dining hall, medical quarters, a line of inmates walking along the fence to report to their different jobs. The Sumter prison is an incentivized facility, so all of the prisoners had to earn their way here with a record of good behavior. There's a variety of sports and activities to keep them busy — flag football, bocce ball, beach volleyball, horseshoes, softball — and the inmates keep track of sports schedules and offerings with their prison-issued tablet.

Randy Puryear, 62, plays pickleball seven days a week. Before prison, he was a dentist and an avid tennis player. He was convicted of second-degree murder in 2002 and given a 25-year sentence, and he found himself desperate for any hint of normalcy.

Puryear peppered BelAir with questions, eager to understand some nuances and learn how pickleball is played on the outside. BelAir told the group about "the kitchen" — the area near the net — and walked them through the scoring. And then he told the inmates his favorite part of the game — the "group hug," in which players all tap their paddles together following a match. "I think it's real simple," BelAir told them. "The world would be a better place if we had more group hugs and less violence."

David Colon, the Sumter warden, watched from the side of the court. He's occasionally picked up a paddle and hit the ball around with the inmates. Some of the other prison sports are dominated by cliques, he says — the Hispanic inmates gravitate to soccer, for example, or many of the Black prisoners stick to the basketball court.

"This is for everybody," Colon said.

BelAir liked the energy and camaraderie he saw on the Sumter courts. Even the newcomers seemed to pick it up quickly.

"You guys are pretty good. Just need more practice," he told them. "Listen, do we have any final questions?"

Gary Tillman, 60, wiped the sweat off his forehead. "When they gonna bring that $2 million tournament in here? I heard about that," said Tillman, who's serving a life sentence for murder. "Tell them we got some players up in here. And we need the money."

BelAir estimates that he's introduced the game to more than 800 inmates. At the conclusion of a visit, he leaves behind the balls, paddles and nets. He wants facilities to make pickleball a permanent offering, as Dart did in Cook County.

On his Florida visit, BelAir taught the sport to more than 300 inmates. From the prisons' perspective, the pickleball tour had been such a success that department officials were already brainstorming how to get the sport into all of the state's facilities, which would make pickleball accessible to thousands of inmates statewide. "We're absolutely going to explore the expansion of pickleball throughout our system," said Mahoney.

BelAir returned home and was already lining up his next trips — eager to introduce the game to Ohio's prison system and then back to California, where he'd take the sport into the San Quentin and Folsom prisons.

"I was asked the other day, how big is this going to get? And my answer is, I don't know," he said. "I take it one step at a time, but I remind myself that Johnny Appleseed started with one apple."

A Pickleball Background Like No Other!

Years ago Roger BelAir was introduced to to Barney McCallum, the only living founder. They quickly became friends and many of the anecdotes and vignettes Roger shares about the game come directly from Barney. Next Roger came to know the managment of Pickle-Ball, Inc., the company formed by the three founders to promote the game. He learned even more "behind the scenes" stories.

As a result, Roger's clinics are uncopyable! With a style that mixes humor, insights, and proper technique, Roger has taught 2,500+ people ... from a former Wimbledon tennis pro to Fortune 500 executives to grandmothers who want to stay active and have fun. He is frequently the Guest Teaching Pro at the renowned Rancho La Puerta (one of the "Five Best Destination Spas in the World" according to Travel + Leisure magazine). He has also taught at the JW Marriott Palm Desert, one of the top ten tennis resorts in the country.

Inspired by a CBS's "60 Minutes" segment on crime, Roger envisioned pickleball as a means of teaching "life skills" in prisons. Since most inmates are eventually released, perhaps pickleball could help make them better people ... making it safer for all of us once they return to society.

His thinking was correct. He introduced the game to men charged with murder at Chicago's Cook County Jail and his program was hugely successful. Gang members who wouldn't even talk to each other were playing pickleball together. Soon they were even laughing together! Disciplinary problems at the jail were reduced.

The success of his program in Chicago led Roger to prisons coast-to-coast, from Rikers Island in New York to Corcoran in California (where Charles Manson served time). His life-changing efforts have been applauded by the Washington Post, NPR, and a front-page story in USA TODAY. A documentary is currently in production.

Off the court, Roger is a financial expert who has been profiled in a cover story of *Money* magazine; an acclaimed author of books on finance and investments; and a keynoter at business conventions around the country. He's been quoted in the *Wall Street Journal*, *New York Times*, and many other publications.

He knows finance, but pickleball is his passion.

Based on all the information that has been presented in this chapter, I believe within the next several years, pickleball will become the dominant/major racquet sport because of its tremendous growth nationwide.

The Wall Street Journal recently included an article titled "John McEnroe Is Playing Pickleball for $1 Million? You Cannot Be Serious." According to the article, "The irascible tennis legend joins Andre Agassi, Andy Roddick and Michael Chang on the pickleball court Sunday [April 2, 2023] with seven figures on the line. But the soul of this sport is its grassroots." These four will compete for $1 million dollars! It will be the highest paid tournament to date!

(wsj.com)

Uniquely Me
By God's Design

A Tragedy Never to be Forgotten

In the midst of a quiet Sunday morning, an explosion, eardrum-shattering loud, rang through the air. Horror filled the hearts of everyone who was in earshot. What was it? What had just occurred?

People began running in all directions, trying to save themselves and help others, while frantically searching for loved ones. Dust blew everywhere as walls crumbled and the floor caved in. Screams and cries rang out, permeating the air. An eeriness surrounded everyone.

The racially-motivated hate group known as the Ku Klux Klan had struck again. At that time, racial tension in the South was extremely high, and Black people had ramped up the Civil Rights Movement with Dr. Martin Luther King, Jr. and the Southern Christian Leadership Conference leading the charge, along with Malcolm X and his supporters. Black people had grown tired and weary of the hate-filled attacks on their property and upon their person. They would remain silent no longer. But, each time they raised their voices in protest, another attack was issued against them.

That Sunday morning, September 15, 1963, before the choir could begin lifting their angelic voices in praise, worship, and adoration to the Lord, a bomb had been detonated. The enormous blast caused physical damage to the church coupled with injury to approximately twenty individuals. The injuries included bruises, sprains, cuts, broken bones, etc. But the most devastating and memorable tragedy was the loss of the lives of four innocent young girls who were not responsible for the acts of discrimination, bigotry, and racism that swept through the Southland like a parasite.

The bombing took place at the Sixteenth Street Baptist Church, taking the precious lives of Denise McNair, Cynthia Wesley, Carole Robertson, and Addie Mae Collins. In the blink of an eye, they had their futures violently snatched away by the hate-filled, cowardly act that was intended as a warning against continuing the fight toward ending segregation and racial inequality.

(Ferris State University, 2022)

The Sixteenth Street Baptist Church was predominately attended by African Americans, and many of its members were active in the ongoing civil rights campaign in Birmingham, Alabama (Ferris State University, 2022). They had desired change, and they were working earnestly toward that end.

That tragic incident rocked the Black community of Birmingham, Alabama as well as many other communities throughout America. I was only eight years old at the time, and receiving the news was devastating. One of the four girls, Denise McNair was quite familiar to me. Her father Chris McNair, who was a photographer, was well known throughout our community. Regardless of my relationship with the four girls, I (like the rest of Birmingham) was impacted by the devastation of such a cruel, senseless act. It is a tragedy I will always remember. It was a tragedy that would serve as a stitch in the fabric of who I would become.

Coming Into My Own

Being born in the mid 1950s and growing up in the 1960s in the deep South was not the easiest feat as a person of color, a minority, and a young girl who would blossom into a woman. But, the favor of God rested upon me, allowing me to have the guidance, love, and encouragement of my wonderful parents who steered me in the right direction. Both my parents were encouragers and great supporters while being humorous and light hearted.

One of the most poignant phrases my parents uttered on a regular basis was, "Lynn, you can do anything you want to do." As they spoke words of encouragement, they taught me many life lessons, such as the importance of loving God, myself, life, and people. From my parents' example, I soon learned love, in and of itself, allowing me to give of myself with a heart filled with kindness.

The Gift of a Mother

Catherine Paulding, or Miss Cat as many called her, was my mother. She and her sisters attended a small church (New Hope Baptist Church) in Bessemer, Alabama. They sang in the choir, while at times being the complete choir. Oh, how they loved to sing praises unto the Lord! My mother was a strong believer in God, and she loved Him with her entire heart. And to learn more about God's Word, she would often take classes. Through her studies, she became a staunch advocate of Apostle Paul.

Mom's love for the Lord caused her to be at church often; if she could have been at church ten days a week, she would have. For my mother, along with loving the Lord came the love of helping people, specifically making sure they had a hearty meal to eat, especially if they were facing a particular condition, such as joblessness or hospitalization. My mother was consistently taking food everywhere, feeding everyone. I guess it was a good thing she was a great cook.

Dedicated to God, church, and God's people, she served as a Sunday school teacher and did whatever was needed in the church. As a mother and homemaker, she ensured all of her children were in church right alongside of her each week. My father was her ally, making sure we were there as well. Not only was my mother very spiritual, but she was also very practical. From my mother's understanding of human nature, she always said, "People are not perfect; therefore, do not view people as though they are hypocrites. Don't live your life criticizing people." She elected to find the good in people rather than being a judgmental person, always taking the high road and treating them better than they sometimes deserved due to their conduct.

Her philosophy was if you find something good in someone, you can build the person up, using the good as a pivoting point. Also, she pointed out people do not receive enough compliments and that people should help one another more. I must admit I did not always understand her philosophy, but as I grew older and matured, I began to see her perspective. Today, even when I know someone may be doing something harmful towards me, I just smile. However, I believe it is wise to address important issues rather than avoid them. However, it must be the right time to do so to keep the situation from going awry. Approaching someone in the heat of the moment can lead to the person being mistreated. Mother would ask, "Can we deal with this at another time?" To keep tempers at bay and to retain the proper perspective, I have adopted her philosophy about treating people with respect and finding the good in them. Furthermore, as a result of my mother, my love for the Lord is strong, and even when I am traveling, I will always find a church to worship God and fellowship with His people.

The Strength of a Father

My father Aaron Paulding was a quiet man with a beautiful personality, who was named after his father and grandfather. And while he believed in God, he was not as heavily into the Word like my mother. Nevertheless, he loved that his wife was a strong Christian and supported her and their children's church attendance and activities.

At one time, he had served in the United States Navy. His brothers, who were his only siblings, had the same proclivity. They served in various branches of the United States Armed Forces. After my father's years of service in the Navy, being a proud man and a hard worker, he worked in the coal mines and at the steel plant.

Outside of the workplace, he always kept his hands busy, making this and that. If something needed repair, he did it. If something did not exist, he made it. He was quite creative and inventive. For example, one day it was raining, and guests were visiting us in our home. He made something for them to wipe their wet shoes on to keep the floors from getting tracked with heavy amounts of debris and water.

Dad was also a person who did everything in a timely manner; better yet, he was the early bird. He was usually nearly an hour early for each activity that was on his daily schedule. For example, if he was to start a job at five in the morning, he would arrive an hour early and be there around four. When his employer learned of that particular character trait by seeing him standing outside on several occasions, they gave him the key to open up, knowing he would be the first to arrive.

As a family man, a husband and father of six children, he provided very well for all of us. If there was anything we needed, he was dedicated to making sure we had it. As a result of his hardworking nature and the absence it caused in my life, I did not have an opportunity to get to know the depths of him. However, amidst his work and our busy adolescent lives, he kept up with his family's activities, and the two of us had a nice father-daughter relationship. Anytime someone inquired about my siblings and my wellbeing, my dad would respond, "They are eating well and sleeping well. They are doing okay." He judged our wellbeing by *what* we were doing.

A part of my father's protective and caring nature was that of a disciplinarian. He believed in order and having well-behaved children. So, when one child misbehaved, he disciplined us all, even those who may have been too young to participate in the activities he believed were deserving of correction. I can recall times when I was with my elder siblings (I am the youngest) while they were engaging in "teenage" activities. Upon our arrival home, we would all be disciplined even though I was "taken" along with them and was not an actual participant in their activities. I complained and whined about being punished too. But, my father was adamant that we would all receive the same treatment.

Another life situation that caused difficulty in spending much quality time with my father was his health. During my high school days, my father suffered from a respiratory condition and subsequently passed away. Although his presence in our home was missed, his life lessons would always stick with us, such as maintaining our solidarity through whatever we experienced.

My Siblings

Together, my parents gave birth to six children, giving me four older sisters and one older brother. Barbara Pruitt was the oldest and is deceased. She was always supportive of me and very kind and encouraging. She would always say, "Lynn, go on with your life," encouraging me to do all that was within my heart to do. My brother, my father's namesake, Aaron Paulding, was the only son amidst five daughters has also passed on. He was the comedian in the family, making everyone laugh. I did not really get a chance to know him well because he moved away to Detroit, Michigan after high school.

Next in succession is my sister Marilyn Paulding, who currently resides in Birmingham, Alabama. She is a great hair stylist and had her own business. I learned my different hairstyles from her. Then, there is Isabell Cotrell, who I followed to Booker T. Washington Business College, learning about the school as a result of her attendance there. She currently resides in the Dallas, Texas area. She and her husband were at the helm of Pro-Line Hair Care Products, a Black hair care company. Her husband was the president, and she worked directly alongside him.

Then, the sister who was born directly before me is Mary Samuel, who currently resides in Bessemer, Alabama. At one point, she worked with Isabell at Pro-Line. She is my personal outfitter, knowing how to select my outfits better than I do. She sends me the most gorgeous gowns and dresses, and they fit perfectly. I thank God for all of my siblings' support and love as well as that of my other relatives.

Marriage

William and I met in Birmingham, Alabama at a Dr. King celebration that was held in a movie theater. I was in line with family and friends at the concession stand getting popcorn. Coming up alongside of me, William asked, "Can I get you some popcorn?" I responded, "We are getting our own popcorn." Not long after that day, we lost contact, but we reconnected later. Then, I went off to school, but he would come visit. After dating for a period, we were married. William loves the Lord and demonstrates his love through singing gospel and being involved in church. We are very compatible, enjoying the same activities, especially outdoor activities in which we engaged often. For example, we snow skied together and went on vacation in Jamaica. We are both very adventurous. We also enjoy worshipping the Lord and bringing in the New Year at church. After some time, our marriage ended in an amicable divorce; and, we still talk on occasion.

The Gift of Others

As a youth, I internalized my parents' words, believing I could achieve anything to which I set my mind. At the same time though, my parents were not naïve regarding the cruelty of the world in which we were presently situated, and while they wanted me to be cognizant of the incredulous demeanors of others that would inevitably be projected toward me, they wanted me to understand no one could stop my progress in life, except me. Yes, there were certainly barriers to cross and hurdles to leap over, but with my spirit of determination and my faith in God, I was well on my way, as my life had a formidable foundation.

My parents also taught me the importance of timeliness, being prompt for scheduled activities, completing tasks in a timely manner, and being respectful of others' time as well as my own. Learning the value of time assisted in my studies, my level of professionalism, and in garnering the respect of my peers, clients and friends and others with whom I came in contact. Time is a precious commodity provided to us by God, and it should not be squandered.

Utilizing my parents' wisdom and guidance as tools to navigate my formative years, I lived the life of the average teenager who possessed an interest in academics, friends, family, church, and tennis, while forging my place within my community. While in high school, I frequented local parks in Birmingham, Alabama and schools (particularly Davis Middle School in Bessemer, Alabama where I resided), to hit the tennis ball around the court with whomever happened to be there at the time.

On occasion at Ensley Park, Mr. James Lewis would be there. He loved the game and did not mind giving me a tennis lesson to cultivate my talent. My parents were right there encouraging me because they witnessed the sheer delight I experienced when I held the racket in my hands.

When I was an adolescent, Mr. Lewis was one of the people who took an interest in me and many other youth who loved the game of tennis. He took time from his schedule to teach us the game, giving us practice lessons as we developed our skills. It was because of him and a few others who helped lay my foundation of tennis. I was one of the individuals who recommended the current non-profit James Lewis tennis foundation in the mid 90's to help the advance of tennis in minority communities.

Impressive, Powerful Women

As a young impressionable girl, not only did my parents' words, lifestyle, and behaviors shaped my life, but the lives, actions, and words of political figures greatly impacted my life as well. Barbara Jordan, who was a lawyer, educator, and politician, served as a great source of inspiration for me. She was the first African American elected to the Texas Senate after Reconstruction and the first Southern African-American woman elected to the United States House of Representatives. As an educator, she taught at a university in Dallas, Texas. I was impressed by her achievements in both the educational and political arenas. She definitely inspired me to reach for and achieve my dreams.

Barbara Jordan
(en.wikipedia.org)

Coupled with Barbara Jordan, Shirley Chisholm was another inspirational political figure. She was an American politician, who became the first black woman to be elected to the United States Congress, in 1968. Chisholm represented New York's 12th congressional district, for seven terms from 1969 to 1983. In 1972, she became the first black candidate to receive a major-party nomination for president of the United States and was the first woman to run for the Democratic Party's nomination.

Shirley Chisholm
(womenshistory.org)

Anytime I had an opportunity to listen to Shirley Chisholm speak, I listened intently because she always spoke from her heart and in the interest of the American people. One phrase in particular uttered by Chisholm captured my attention: "If they don't give you a seat at the table, bring a folding chair." Her words spoke volumes to me, letting me know people may not include me in their discussions or decision-making processes. Despite that truth, I have the power, ability, and authority to enter the conversation at will. So, whether or not I am invited into the dialogue, I can make the choice to enter the discussion of my own volition.

Both Jordan and Chisholm sparked hope within me because they served as real-life examples of strong, powerful Black women who had and were making their mark in the world. Seeing them in action gave me more reason to believe what my parents had been saying to me my entire life. And, it was primarily because of these two women, amongst other inspirational and historical figures, that propelled me into a life of politics. Furthermore, with all I had witnessed in my community and those surrounding it, I desired to represent Black people, being a much-needed voice during a time where our voices were few and the call to action was dire.

The Impact of a King

Another inspirational figure in my life whose own life spoke volumes to me was Dr. Martin Luther King, Jr. who was both an advocate for civil rights and a minster of the gospel of Jesus Christ. Dr. King was a giant of a man with a large personality who impacted the lives of many – those who lived during his lifetime and many, many more who have come after. His advocacy for others and his dedication to going to lengths only imagined by others is awe inspiring, especially knowing his plight cost him his very life. But, it was certainly not a life that was lived in vain. He was ordained by God for his life mission and was vastly used therein. He answered the call, and he fought the good fight of faith using the vision God had given him.

While a portion of Dr. King's notoriety came from his infamous "I Have a Dream Speech," he made many poignant statements that were life impacting. One famous question he asked that lingers in my spirit is, "What is your life's blueprint?" Repeating his question in my mind periodically over my life, I often question myself as I ponder over my life. Today, 54 years after his assassination, his words and that particular question are still remembered and being discussed.

It was "six months before he was assassinated, [when] King spoke to a group of students at Barratt Junior High

School in Philadelphia on October 26, 1967" when he asked the question. To answer the question himself, he continued by saying, "Whenever a building is constructed, you usually have an architect who draws a blueprint, and that blueprint serves as the pattern, as the guide, and a building is not well erected without a good, solid blueprint. Now each of you is in the process of building the structure of your lives, and the question is whether you have a proper, a solid and a sound blueprint. I want to suggest some of the things that should begin your life's blueprint. Number one in your life's blueprint, should be a deep belief in your own dignity, your worth, and your own somebodiness. Don't allow anybody to make you feel that you're nobody. Always feel that you count. Always feel that you have worth, and always feel that your life has ultimate significance" (from the Estate of Dr. Martin Luther King, Jr., printed courtesy of the Seattle Times, 2017).

Rev. Martin Luther King, Jr.
(Martin Mills/Getty Images)

With such strong political leaders having blazed a trial before me, by the time I graduated high school, I possessed a strong desire to attend college to pursue a degree in political science. It was my fervent belief that a background in political science, a certified education, and a heart of compassion would allow me to navigate the political arena, thereby empowering me for the tasks that lay ahead. By watching Jordan and Chisholm, I learned how to carry myself, how to speak out regarding my beliefs and political stances, and to push forward through adversity as an agent of change. With the arsenal I was mentally preparing to equip myself with, I anticipated doors opening in my future, whereby I could be instrumental in effectuating change for Black people by assisting in eradicating laws that served as barriers to progress.

Forging My Own Path

In the mental landscape of my mind, I envisioned my future. However, I did not anticipate the absence of my father, the one who had shouldered the responsibility of our family. Unfortunately, my father would not be by my side as I graced the graduation stage to receive my high school diploma. Nor would he be with me as I prepared to take my first college course. Sadly, he passed away during my senior year of high school. And although my heart was broken, I would forever carry his encouraging words with me, allowing them to continue to steer and guide me along my journey. My mother, though, was with me every step of the way, just as she had always been. With her continued encouragement and physical presence and the benefits from the Veteran's Administration, I was able to attend college.

Transitioning from high school to college was without difficulty as I had always been a hard-working academic, loving the process of learning and engaging with the knowledge I obtained. However, there had been one major disruption during my formative education but in the end, it served as a benefit.

In 1970, I experienced school integration as a freshman attending Jess Lanier High School in Bessemer, Alabama. Never before had I attended school with White classmates. In the midst of the integration efforts, I was able to witness a marked difference between the education White students had received from elementary school through junior high versus the education I and my counterparts had received. From my observations, the White students in my classes where educationally advanced. As a result, I increased my study time by two to three hours daily to ensure my education was up to par with the current standards. I was not in competition with the White students, but because I was suddenly being held to a different standard than I had been, I was determined to meet or exceed every expectation the school system was placing upon me.

Today, viewing the situation in retrospect, I am reminded of Plessy v Ferguson, which instituted "separate but equal" schooling in 1894. That ruling had been overturned in 1954 with Brown v Board of Education, which stated "separate" does not automatically ensure "equal" educational protection under the law. However, it took another sixteen years after the Supreme Court ruling for a change to be instituted in my school district. Therefore, my education and that of my counterparts had been affected. While I was fortunate to have the understanding that I needed to enact personal changes to be able to withstand the new classroom challenges, the same was not true for many other students, which eventually led to some of them not completing courses, which unfortunately meant no graduation and no high school diploma.

That significant experience was yet another catalyst for opening my eyes wider to the current position I held of the world and how the world saw me as an individual- a young Black woman. Prior to that occurrence, there had been many other happenings that allowed me to obtain clarity about the mistreatment of Blacks and their unequal footing in American society. For example, I witnessed segregation between Blacks and Whites by use of signs that stated "White Only" and "Colored," a term I despised, in restaurants and store windows. Use of signs to restrict direct access was minor compared to the events that extinguished the lives of Black people.

It was collectively experiencing several incidents like that one, witnessing educational disparity amongst Blacks and Whites first hand, admiring the progressive careers of Barbara Jordan and Shirley Chisholm, and receiving motivation from my parents that developed an unquestionable resolve within me to rise up and use my God-given voice to effectuate change in our modern-day society as it related to equality amongst all people in all areas of life by ensuring Black people had a platform to voice their collective concerns.

The Collegiate Experience

In the Fall of 1974, after graduating high school, I began attending Booker T. Washington Business College, which was owned by the entrepreneur and philanthropist Dr. Arthur George Gaston and his wife, Minnie Gardener Gaston. I enrolled in and completed business courses over the next two years.

Booker T. Washington Business College
(encyclopediaofalabama.org)

In the summer of 1976, I transferred to Tuskegee Institute (now called Tuskegee University) and enrolled in the Bachelor of Science program focusing on Political Science. I was able to transfer the credits I earned at Booker over to Tuskegee. That summer held unexpected excitement. While surveying the campus, I heard the familiar sound of tennis balls flying through the air and hitting the ground. I also heard voices and laughter. Excited by the possibility of engaging in my favorite pastime, I joined a game and quickly made friends.

Not long afterward, I met the tennis coach who had been watching as I played. He walked up to me and said, "You are on the team." I had never been on a tennis team before, so imagine my excitement. But, there was another problem- I did not actually know the rules of the game. All the years prior, I had just hit the ball around with friends and people from my community. But, as it turned out, I did not need to concern myself with my lack of knowledge. The coach assigned people to work with me and teach me the rules. Their guidance helped me advance from playing at a decent level to becoming a knowledgeable player.

As I took classes and learned about Political Science, I also practiced the game of tennis and played in matches against high dignitaries (Black and White) for fun and against other Historically Black Colleges and Universities (HBCUs) for the official record in district competitions. Our team also played against a few White colleges for skill. However, those games were for competition only, not for the official record.

While enrolled at Tuskegee, I developed as an individual (intellectually, physically, and emotionally). There was much occurring around me that broadened my consciousness while learning on a daily basis in the midst of my peers. For example, I was able to engage with prominent Black people who reached out to other Blacks to provide additional support while they were in the midst of attaining higher education.

One particular group was the Commodores, of which the pop icon Lionel Richie was the first lead. All members of the group had been students at Tuskegee in their youth, and Richie had actually been "raised on the campus of Tuskegee University where two preceding generations of his family had worked" (Key, 2018). His love and dedication to the Tuskegee Institute led him to continuously return to the campus and interact with the students, particularly the students who played tennis. He purchased new tennis rackets for the players and even played a few games with us. As an alumnus of the university, Lionel Richie returned there often to give back and help build the college's legacy. William King, another member of the Commodores, also played tennis with us on occasion. Having these men share their time and talent in a game that was dear to our hearts was memorable.

While engaging in all Tuskegee had to offer from the classroom to the tennis courts, relishing in the comradery of the professors to the fellow students, and appreciating encouragement from alumni, I earned a Bachelor of Science degree in Political Science in 1979.

Nearly one year later, I enrolled in Southern University for approximately a year to further my study of American law, before transferring to the University of Alabama. During that time of study, my focus was strictly on my educational journey. Tennis had truly become an activity of leisure, being played only on the occasional weekend and holidays.

Attending the University of Alabama was a different experience than Tuskegee, Southern, and Booker T. Washington. In my earlier experiences with higher education, most of the students were of African descent. However, during my postgraduate studies at the University of Alabama, there were only seven to eight Black students enrolled in each of my courses, and most were the offspring of medical doctors and lawyers. However, I did not permit their elitist status (or rather that of their parents) to be a factor of intimidation. Rather, I approached each course as I always had- as a learning opportunity. My peers were seen as resources, just as the members of the faculty. I learned from all of them and in turn, I shared my knowledge with them. Many of my peers were intellectually gifted; from my perspective, they were the crème of the crop. The way I saw it, we were all traveling along the same journey and had an expected end. My objective, as was theirs, was to reach the end success-fully.

During those two years, I developed my oratorical skills, as the professors expected students to be prepared to provide case details at a moment's notice, demon-strating their knowledge of each case being studied and how those details impacted current laws and/or new cases that could be brought before the court. Furthermore, impromptu speaking was a welcomed challenge as it enhanced my debating skills, which were required as a member of the university's debate team. I had always been loquacious, and what better way to put my gift of gab to use?

While mastering my craft of courtroom etiquette, gaining case knowledge, and learning applicable termi-nology, I also continued to survey the world around me, watching race relations develop or stagnate. As I deemed appropriate, I joined the conversation when the opportu-nity presented itself. For example, I had one opportunity (of many) while engaging in a rare occasion of a game of tennis to enlighten a young Black boy of ten or eleven years of age. He was the son of one of the few Black professors at University of Alabama. He was an excellent tennis player who was overflowing with zeal for both the game and life in general. And, at his young age, he unfortunately held the false belief that the world viewed all humans as equal, with equal rights, protections, and opportunities. I ascertained his hopeful mindset when he shared with me the details of his impending trip to a country club. He told me one of his friends had invited him as his personal guest. Obviously, he and his friend thought it would be a grand idea to attend together.

However, because the young boy had not yet visited the club, I knew his chances of actually going were slim to none. In an effort to assist in shaping his reality and understanding about the current state of the world in regards to race relations, I explained to him that his friend truly wanted him to be his personal guest; however, the current rules of engagement for that particular establishment may not permit him to grace the premises due to the color of his skin.

It was disheartening for me to be required to assist someone in understanding the inequities of life. It caused me to have to stop and face yet another constant reminder of the imbalances that plagues our country. As disheartened as I may have been, I would not be deterred from attempting to achieve my personal goal of assisting Blacks in their personal endeavors and to ensure justice prevailed within legal battles. With the heavy burden I carried in my heart, I understood the necessity of pressing forward in my educational endeavors because as far as I was concerned, the status quo of societal inequities could not remain.

Early in 1983, as I pressed onward in my studies at the University of Alabama, two or three African American civil rights lawyers came to the campus to speak to some of the law students. They wanted to inform us of employment opportunities that could potentially be available at the Legal Services Department as well as with their law practices in Selma, AL after we graduated. I was intrigued by the possibility of working in that capacity, so I, along with some of my peers, filed the information away in my mind for a later time. That time came the next year.

In 1984, at the culmination of my years of study at the University of Alabama, I earned a Juris Doctorate. Afterward, I began to search for employment. Remembering the information the civil rights attorneys had shared with us, I applied for a legal assistant position at the Legal Services Department and was subsequently hired. So, there I was in Selma, Alabama assisting in the civil rights' arena where my passion lay. I was employed there for over two years, until I was hired as in investigator with the Equal Employment Opportunity Commission (EEOC) in 1987.

A Search for the Truth

As an investigator, it was my responsibility to investigate complaints of discrimination and/or misconduct supposedly perpetrated against employees by the companies that employed them. These complaints ranged across a broad spectrum of categories, from racism, to sexism, to ageism, to disability discrimination, to issues of diversity and inclusion. When employees filed grievance claims, I was responsible for speaking to them to hear their concerns as a means of beginning to gather evidence. If I determined the complaints had merit, I would then build a case on the person's behalf. By that point, most of the complainants were no longer employed by the company. It was a challenging, yet rewarding job.

I investigated employee grievances for a period of three or four years, until I moved to Atlanta, Georgia and became an employee of the United States Tennis Association (USTA). My specific assignment in the USTA was to integrate tennis from being a sport that was dominated by European Americans to one that embraced all ethnicities. I was intrigued by the possibilities of the job, but little did I know I would be fighting an uphill battle.

Impactful Celebs

Oprah Winfrey

Around 2003, I began journaling. This is a practice I learned while watching Oprah Winfrey and listening to her share keen wisdom with the viewing audience. As a technique for us to remain humble, while possessing a spirit of gratitude, Oprah advised us to compose a list of five blessings every day. For me, the list is a tangible method for being reminded of what God has done and is doing to bless me. I took her advice, and I have been journaling my list of blessings. As of today, nearly every morning for approximately twenty years, I have composed a list of blessings. Oftentimes, my list exceeds Oprah's recommendation of five, numbering between 10-20 blessings. Taking Oprah's advice and putting it into practice has been profoundly life changing, and for that I am grateful.

As a result of creating this tangible list that I can see and hold, I am reminded of God's love for me and the numerous blessings He has bestowed in my life. More importantly, my gratitude has increased, leading me to become a kinder person, one who treats other people with kindness and respect. My overall disposition is a representation of I Corinthians 13:13 (NLT), *"Three things will last forever—faith, hope, and love—and the greatest of these is love."* I possess these attributes to a greater degree, as they have come to give my life shape and develop an attitude of thanksgiving within me, giving me a newfound respect for daily living. Thus, on a daily basis, I display these attributes towards my heavenly Father and towards my fellow humans, and it is all due to a nugget of wisdom Oprah took the time to share with all who would grasp hold of it.

(discountmags.com)

Tyler Perry

Tyler Perry is a world-renowned producer, director, actor, screenwriter, playwright, author, songwriter, entrepreneur, and philanthropist. His life story, sharing all he has endured and overcome coupled with his generous heart, causes me to have a tremendous amount of respect and admiration for him. And although "preacher" is not typically in his list of titles/positions, I consider him to be a preacher in his own right having heard him render the Word of God in a clear, concise, and accurate manner.

Furthermore, the wealth he has amassed (reaching billionaire status) despite his previous lifestyle is both remarkable and encouraging.

Warren Buffet

Another billionaire whose life is a source of encouragement is Warren Buffet, an American business magnate, investor, and philanthropist "who is widely considered the most successful investor of the 20th century. He has amassed a personal fortune of more than $60 [fluid] billion by defying prevailing investment trends" (Encyclopedia Britannica, 2023). Even with a current net worth of over $100 billion, he makes being a billionaire look simplistic, which is a very rare and unique trait for someone who is rich and famous. His life is so incredibly intriguing that I would one day like to attend one of his conferences to learn more from him. Interestingly, Buffet lives in the same house in Omaha, Nebraska that he has lived in for quite some time. He believes in keeping life simple regardless of the amount of wealth he has accumulated.

(businesstoday.in, 2023)

A Family that Prays Together

For me, education is a great foundation and tool for everyday living, and it certainly helps with personal employment aspirations. But, having faith in the Almighty God is crucial to living a balanced life in that as a spiritual being who is functioning in the natural arena, I must be well grounded as it relates to the three parts of me: spirit, soul, and body. Having developed a belief in God and a strong faith in His Word, something that was fortified during my youth, I have had several prayer partners throughout my life.

As I mentioned earlier, my father had passed away while I was in high school. God saw fit to provide me with the love, guidance, and care of another father in the person of Mr. Robert Long, a great man of God from Birmingham, Alabama, who served as my godfather. I had met Mr. Long and his wife when I was attending Booker T. Washington and visited with them approximately two to three times a week. When the time came for me to be joined in holy matrimony, I asked if he would do the honors of giving me away at the wedding, and although he was delighted to do so, he unfortunately was in the hospital at that time in 2001. My brother graciously filled in for him and was proud to walk me down the aisle.

I admired Mr. Long and his wife Mrs. Jackie Long, for they truly loved the Lord and treated me like a daughter. Living life on the lighter side, they were both true comedians and kept me in stitches with their humor. Having Mr. Long in my life gave me the experience of knowing and having a father after my first father had passed, and for that, I will always be grateful. With him in my life, I was able to enjoy the blessings of a father once again, until his passing around the age of 90.

On occasion, I reminisce about the moments I shared with Mr. and Mrs. Long. I remember the immense affection and respect he had for his wife. To demonstrate his deep love and admiration for her, he addressed her as Mrs. Long, rather than by her first name as most husbands tend to do. I was in awe of that particular practice as I had never witnessed it in operation before. I suspect for him, giving her his name on their wedding day and using it when he called out to her or spoke of her made her truly a part of him. So, he treated her with the utmost respect just as he treated himself. She was his queen, and he treated her as such.

Next was my godmother, Mother Rowland, whom I met in Atlanta in 1991-2. She was a mentor to me, a Sunday school teacher, and a Bible study teacher. She held a very special place in my life as my godmother. I could call her at any time as she truly was a mother to me. I learned quite a bit from her, about God, about prayer (as she was a praying lady), and about life from the conversations we had every other day. I still value her input and her wisdom, and I will always keep her advice with me even though she is no longer here. She passed from this life in 2022 at the age of 105. During that time, I met a wonderful woman who became a good friend who always lends a listening ear: Jeanette Myles (owner/clothes designer of Myles Creations in Atlanta, GA). We have been good friends for over 25 years.

Another formidable woman in my life with whom I shared much prayer time was Sister Cooley. In years past, she had helped to raise my mother and her siblings. Sis. Cooley was another well-respected woman of God in our community whom I would visit with nearly once a week, and we would sit and talk for several hours. She was a mentor to me after my mother passed away. I knew her husband Mr. James Cooley as well; I had met both of them as a young girl. Both were very nice people and assisted in the community. As a result of Mr. Cooley's work and mark upon the community, a youth development program was named after him. He passed away when I was a young girl, and in 2021-2, Sister Cooley passed at the age of 100.

In San Francisco, at Third Baptist Church, there was a powerful 6am prayer team, and I prayed with them often. Presently, I am on another 6am prayer line, and we pray for not only the personal needs of the group members and their families, but we intercede for our nation and the world at large.

At my former church, Love, Peace, and Happiness Family Christian Fellowship Church, I prayed with some of the prayer warriors there and built relationships. The fellowship and the senior pastor Bishop Leon Martin were loving and kind, welcoming me into their circle of love. Also, Bishop Martin taught me the importance of moving forward and not allowing myself to be debilitated by the occurrences of my life. Although Bishop Martin had opened churches in various locations and oversaw them all, he was not too busy to teach people about controlling their finances, but that is part of his life as a businessman, and he passes his vast knowledge of various topics onto the parishioners. I appreciate how he is able to do so many things, and he teaches others how to go after things in life and to achieve.

Bishop Leon Martin

Along with the aforementioned prayer partners were a pair of prayer warriors I must include in my list of honorable mentions: Mrs. Mary Martin and Mother Foster. Mrs. Mary Martin, whom I met at Tuskegee and lived with for a while, was a great woman of God and an effective prayer warrior. Like my godmother, Mother Rowland, I learned much about life from Mrs. Martin. Mother Foster, whom I met in San Francisco, was like a mother to me. Like most of the others, she has passed away. While living, she and Mrs. Martin had a powerful evangelistic convalescent ministry. Evangelist Ray knew both Mrs. Martin and Mother Foster from their ministry. Evangelist Ray was one praying lady, who would go out to the street and evangelize the lost to Jesus Christ. They were all good friends, and on occasion, I worked with them in their ministry.

Bette Stampley is another powerful woman of God with whom I was able to connect. Minister Bette serves at the Faith Community Baptist Church in Desert Hot Springs, where she resides. Pastor Blaylock is the head pastor. She and her husband were missionaries, traveling around the world spreading God's Word. When I had somewhere to go or something to do, Mrs. Stampley would often say, "I'll go with you, Linda." Furthermore, she provided a place for me to stay overnight when I was in town, prior to my relocation to that area.

Presently, I sometimes attend worship services at New Bethel and participate in their 6am prayer line that is moderated by Mother Butler. Pastor McNeal is the pastor. Additionally, I sometimes worship at The Bridge Church, a Calvary Chapel Church, under the leadership of Pastor Chuck Wooley in Cathedral City. The Bridge Church participates in community outreach and has a program that has been providing aide to Uganda for well over ten years. I have the privilege of assisting with Uganda fundraisers on occasion. Also, I assisted to Pastor Jane at the United Methodist Church in Palm Springs, who has a plethora of programs to help the community, especially the feeding and housing ministry.

There are two pastors, whose worship services are televised, who provide much inspiration, encouragement, and guidance via God's Word: Pastor Joel Olsten and Bishop T. D. Jakes. Joel Olsten is a very powerful motivator. He makes me believe I can do anything. If I desire to run a marathon, after listening to him, I will go out and run the marathon. Bishop Jakes powerfully preaches the Word of God, delivering crown jewels and nuggets as he often provides an exegesis of a particular biblical text. He is an amazing, inspirational pastor. I listen to many of his sermons when I really want to hear an in-depth message on the Word of God. His expertise of God's Word is life changing! Coupling the ministries of Olsten and Jakes together in my life is powerful!

Swinging About the Court
My Love of Tennis

An Ordinary Day

As the breeze brushed against my skin, it warmed the cold beads of sweat that ran freely down my arms and legs. The sky was clear, and the birds chirped overhead as they sat perched in the branches of the nearby trees.

I was euphoric as I experienced the fulness of the zone that had captivated my attention. Pure joy penetrated my core, and a smile spread itself across my face.

As I pivoted on one foot and moved to the right, I quickly shifted and pivoted on the opposite foot and moved to the left. My arms flew up then down, as they swung this way then that. As my pace quickened so did my breathing, for my adrenaline was increasing.

But, there was no one to scream my name to encourage me to push forward. The only people present were my opponent and I. But that was perfectly fine.

All I needed was...

my tennis racket...

a tennis ball...

and, a tennis court...

You see, I was enthralled as I engaged in one of my first loves: tennis!

Yes, I enjoy coaching pickleball and am intrigued about its growth...

Yes, I enjoy working within the political arena effectuating change regarding the civil rights of individuals...

But, tennis is one of my first loves!

Unexpected Turn of Events

Ever since my days of playing tennis as a young child in the parks and school campuses of Bessemer, Alabama, I have absolutely loved and been intrigued by the game of tennis. As a direct result, tennis has been a major part of my life for quite some time. As such, over the course of my life, there have been uncountable times when I have experienced pure joy while engaging in the game of tennis and while coaching others.

Although I had played tennis for entertainment and eventually learned all the rules and became part of a team at the Tuskegee Institute, the day came when my involvement with tennis would shift. In 1991, a unique opportunity was presented to me, allowing me to delve further into the wonderful yet complicated world of tennis.

Dennis Van der Meer, who was the founder and served as the CEO for the United States Professional Tennis Registry (USPTR), which is one of the governing bodies for tennis certifications, recommended me for the position of Minority Participation Coordinator (MPC) with the United States Tennis Association (USTA). The USTA was currently looking for a person of color to head up the Southern Region, which consisted of nine states: Alabama, Mississippi, Georgia, North Carolina, South Carolina, Arkansas, Louisiana, Kentucky, and Tennessee, of which John Callen was the executive director. He was the one who hired me and during my time of employment, he served as a good mentor.

My affiliation with Van der Meer had come from my attendance at his Tennis University program (a tennis camp), which was held in South Carolina several years before. At that time, his program was unique in comparison to others in that it incorporated women and minorities, ensuring both sexes of various races and ethnicities would be included in tennis. The current Executive Director/CEO of the USPTR is Dan Santorum, who is a visionary leader, who immediately jumped on pickleball before the other licensing bodies.

I accepted the position of Minority Participation Coordinator, promoting and recruiting minority tennis players, making me the first person holding the position in the Southern region. Accepting the position came with the requirement of residing in Atlanta, Georgia, so I packed my belongings and relocated.

Working in the position was extremely rewarding because I was able to travel throughout the South, meeting with a variety of organizations and tennis players who had a desire to increase their engagement within the tennis organization but who were having difficulty doing so for a number of reasons, mostly lacking the knowledge of what to do. As the MPC, it was my job to help those players by providing relevant information about the USTA's regulatory guidelines as well as break through barriers that stifled their progress with entering into organized tournaments as constructed and overseen by the USTA.

Another reward of my position was having an expense account that allowed me to travel and conduct the required business without concern or worry that the budget had to be preapproved before I could travel and attend to my duties. While traveling and moving from airport to hotel to events with the purpose of meeting with aspiring tennis players who were in a particular location, I could rent cars, reserve hotel rooms, eat at very nice restaurants, and even treat my 'clients' to lunch during our business meetings without specific regard to the budget. All associated fees were absorbed into my expense account. The USTA's sizable budget was exactly what I needed while reaching out to more and more interested parties who had a genuine interest in the game of tennis. Having a budget without specific constraints assisted greatly in my ability to move about as quickly as I needed.

On some occasions, I would travel to one city one day and be required at another engagement in another city the very next day. On other occasions, I could find myself in two different cities on the same day, sometimes traveling with coworkers to their events where I would meet more people and engage them in a conversation about tennis. That was an additional method for me to offer my services to more individuals. In whatever city I found myself, I enjoyed my high-profile position while visiting some of the most beautiful places in the United States. I was also fortunate to go to the U.S. Open via the USTA's generosity, which was an opportunity of a lifetime for all tennis enthusiasts and players of all levels.

As MPC, I was proffered numerous high-demand requests from many organizations who were well aware of USTA's well-endowed status. They also selected me as a member of their board because they desired a direct connection to the USTA via a USTA employee, whereby they could solicit funding when needed. Although I consented to being on numerous companies' boards, I was far too busy to attend every scheduled board meeting. And, the companies worked with my schedule. My lack of attendance did not harm my seat on the board; all they were concerned with was having the ear of the USTA via a conduit: me. However, once I was no longer with the USTA, my seat on each board would quickly become available without a courtesy warning. Ironically, that exact occurrence had been forewarned years prior by a magnificent woman of God.

Conversely, my new position also came with a few challenges, some bumps in the road I had not anticipated. I soon learned, not long after I was in the position, that although I was hired to promote tennis in the southern region, it would appear that integration of the sport would prove to be a slow realized process. Although it was not directly stated, I often felt as though I was fighting an uphill battle within the organization as it related to my desire to reach out to minority tennis players to provide the representation they needed. Representation equated to a voice who could speak on their behalf and attend to their interests. It was as though I was hired for the position and given the title but not expected to fulfill the requirements of the position. Regardless of the opposition I experienced, I was determined to fully operate in the capacity of which I had been hired. I was hired to recruit individuals into the USTA in an effort to integrate the sport, and I intended to put forth my best effort. It was not an easy experience, but I had been taught to be a fighter and fight I would.

Amidst following through with effectuating my plan, I was often told I had the toughest section to work in due to my geographic region being in the South. I did not allow that viewpoint to deter me either. I was determined to produce and actually earn my salary.

Although tennis had gained its popularity in the 70s and 80s and had been integrated, there were and are very few minority tennis professionals, such as Althea Gibson and Arthur Ashe. Althea Gibson is one of the great players who contributed to making tennis what it is today. While serving in my position of MPC, I was delighted to be able to speak to Gibson by phone on several occasions.

Tennis "Legends & Greats"

In 1940, Althea Gibson won her first tournament, the New York State Championship of the American Tennis Association (ATA), [a Black tennis organization, which has been in existence over 100 years and whom Roxanne Aaron, a tireless leader, is the current president]. All through the 1940s, Gibson won title after title. The ATA gave Gibson ample opportunity to prove her prowess among black tennis players, but it was a limited market. Tennis was a segregated sport at the time; indeed, the ATA itself was expressly organized for blacks who were denied the right to play in the U.S. National Championship competitions (now the U. S. Open). That changed in 1950, largely due to the courage of another woman, Alice Marble, [who stated,] "If tennis is a game for ladies and gentlemen, it's also time we acted a little more like gentlepeople and less like sanctimonious hypocrites. If Althea Gibson represents a challenge to the present crop of women players, it's only fair that they should meet that challenge on the courts." Marble declared that if Gibson wasn't given the opportunity to compete, "then there is an uneradicable mark against a game to which I have devoted most of my life, and I would be bitterly ashamed." Gibson's invitation soon arrived, making her the first black player (male or female) to play at Forest Hills in the sport's national championships. It was her 23rd birthday.

The next six years were peppered with achievements and notoriety for Althea Gibson:

- In 1951, Gibson won her first international title, the Caribbean Championships in Jamaica, and a few months later, she became the first Black person to play at Wimbledon.
- In 1952, she was ranked seventh nationally by the U. S. Tennis Association.
- In 1956, she became the first black athlete to win a Grand Slam singles championship, the French Open; before the year was out, she also won the Wimbledon doubles championship, the Italian national championship, and the Asian championship.
- In July of 1957, she won the world singles championship at Wimbledon and became the first Black person to take the title in the tournament's eight-decade history. Queen Elizabeth personally presented the trophy to an awestruck Gibson. "Shaking hands with the Queen of England," [Gibson] said, "was a long way from being forced to sit in the colored section of the bus." In addition to the top spot in singles at Wimbledon that year, Gibson walked away as the doubles champion, too, for the second year in a row. When she returned to America, she became the second black American (the first being Jesse Owens) honored by a ticker tape parade down Broadway in New York City, with

more than a hundred thousand people cheering their approval.

- Later in 1957, Gibson won the Nationals. Then, in 1958, she successfully defended her Wimbledon and United States titles while also emerging victorious at the Australian Open, giving her no less than three of the four Grand Slam titles in professional tennis. Both in 1957 and in 1958, Althea Gibson was the number one–ranked woman tennis player in the world. Honored as "Female Athlete of the Year" by the Associated Press in both years, she also became the first black woman to appear on the covers of Sports Illustrated and Time magazines.

(Foundation for Economic Education, 2015)

Glenn Giliam of Executive Director Strategic Partnerships is a good friend of mine. Some of the projects he was enthusiastic about was the Althea Gibson Film Project & Screening Tour, Educational Outreach (a DE&I Program), and being the presenter of the Althea Came First Difference Maker Award.

Althea Gibson
(smithsonianmag.com)

Arthur Ashe
(cbsnews.com)

Arthur Ashe, who won the junior national title in 1960 and 1961, is also to be celebrated for making gigantic strides in tennis. In 1963, Ashe was recruited by the U.S. Davis Cup team. In 1968, Ashe captured the U.S. Open title (sponsored by the USTA) as the first and only African American male player to do so.

In 1975, he won Wimbledon, becoming the number one tennis player in the world. In 1985, Ashe was inducted into the International Tennis Hall of Fame and was the first African American male to do so (Biography, 2021). I had an opportunity to meet Ashe at a USPTR conference in South Carolina, where he was teaching pros the back hand technique. He inspired me to become a great coach. He told me, "You are going to be a great coach." I appreciated his kind words and will always remember them.

The well-known tennis superstars Venus Williams, who "made her professional tennis debut in 1994" (Bazaar, 2022) and her younger sister Serena Williams, who made her debut in 1995, are among the minorities. They are/were involved in tennis for "more than 20 years" (Bazaar). They have both won titles in Wimbledon, Australian Open, Summer Olympics, French Open, playing singles and doubles. Furthermore, the Williams sisters have been ranked at the world's number one position by the Women's Tennis Association.

Venus excelled in the following during her tennis career:
- Turning professional in 1994,
- She reached her first major final at the 1997 US Open.
- In 2000 and 2001, Williams claimed the Wimbledon and US Open titles, as well as Olympic singles gold at the 2000 Sydney Olympics.
- She first reached the singles world No. 1 ranking on 25 February 2002, becoming the first African American woman to do so in the Open era, and the second of all-time after Althea Gibson.
- She reached four consecutive major finals between 2002 and 2003, but lost each time to Serena. She then suffered from injuries, winning just one major title between 2003 and 2006.
- Williams returned to form starting in 2007, when she won Wimbledon (a feat she repeated the following year).
- In 2010, she returned to the world No. 2 position in singles, but then suffered again from injuries.

- Starting in 2014, she again gradually returned to form, culminating in two major final appearances at the Australian Open and Wimbledon in 2017.
- Along with her seven singles major titles, Williams has also won 14 women's doubles major titles, all partnering Serena; the pair is unbeaten in Grand Slam doubles finals.
- She became the world No. 1 in doubles for the first time on June 7, 2010, alongside Serena, after the pair completed a non-calendar-year Grand Slam at the French Open.
- The pair also won three Olympic gold medals in women's doubles, in 2000, 2008, and 2012, adding to Venus' singles gold in 2000 and her mixed doubles silver in 2016.
- Williams has also won two mixed doubles major titles, both in 1998.

(Biography, 2022)

Serena's tennis career consists of the following highlights:
- 1995 – Makes her professional debut aged 14 at the Bell Challenge in Quebec City.
- 1998 – Makes Grand Slam main draw debut at Australian Open aged 16. Beats sixth-seed Irina Spirlea but loses in the second round to sister Venus Williams.
- 1998 – Wins first Grand Slam doubles title at Wimbledon in mixed doubles with Croatia's Max Mirnyi.
- 1999 – Beats Swiss legend Martina Hingis in straight sets to win her first Grand Slam singles title at the US Open. On her way to the final, Serena beat

Grand Slam champions Kim Clijsters, Conchita Martínez and Monica Seles.

- 2000 – Bags first Olympic gold along with sister Venus in the women's doubles category.
- 2001 – Her family is marred by controversy as Venus withdraws from the Indian Wells semi-final against Serena and their father claims racial abuse from fans.
- 2002 – Records first French Open and Wimbledon titles, beating Venus in both finals and replacing her as the new world number one.
- 2003 – Completes career Grand Slam (winning all four Grand Slams at least once) by winning her first Australian Open singles title at the age of 22.
- 2005 – Wins her second Australian Open after being out with injury and not winning a Grand Slam since Wimbledon 2003.
- 2012 – Wins Olympic gold in singles and doubles, completing career golden slam.
- 2014 – Exits Wimbledon in the third round for the first time since 2005 and withdraws from her doubles match alongside sister Venus.
- 2015 – Wins third French Open and 20th Grand Slam title, becoming the third person to win each Grand Slam three times. Also wins all four Grand Slams in a row for the second time, the only player to have done so. Returns to Indian Wells after 14 year boycott.

(As a journalist for the Black Tennis Magazine (Marcus Freeman, CEO, former president of ATA), I wrote several articles, including one on Serena's return to Indian Wells.)

Serena's Return To Indian Wells

By Linda Paulding

The fans adorned Indian Wells with signs and excitement. Serena had not played there in 14 years. In fact, the last time she played at the Tennis Garden was in 2001 when she played Kim Clijster in three sets. Serena, Venus and Richard received racial remarks and the crowd was not respectful to this awesome family in 2001. However, Serena has moved forward and felt great about playing this tournament. Additionally, during her triumphant return on March 13, 2015, in tears she played Monica Niculescu at the BNP Paribas Open on Stadium Court 1 and won the match.

Lastly, Serena stated that her decision to return was inspired by Nelson Mandela and forgiveness. She withdrew from the event on Wed. March 18th (semi-final) and stated that she was experiencing problems in her right knee. In fact, she was scheduled to play Halep in the semi-final match.

- 2016 – Wins her seventh and last Wimbledon singles title after dropping just one set during the tournament. Partners sister Venus to win their sixth Wimbledon doubles and 14th overall Grand Slam title together.
- 2017 – Wins her 23rd Grand Slam and seventh Australian Open title by defeating sister Venus in the final. She later announces her pregnancy, making her at least eight weeks pregnant while playing the tournament.

- 2018 – Returns to Grand Slam tennis at French Open but withdraws in the fourth round due to injury.
- 2019 – Loses finals at Wimbledon and US Open.
- 2020 – Wins her first title as a mother at the Auckland Open.
- 2021 – Suffers injury at Wimbledon, withdraws from US Open.
- 2022 – Announces retirement plans in a magazine article, making the US Open her last tournament.

(Serena Williams Timeline, 2022)

Serena edges Venus in surreal Lexington scene

As I persisted in fulfilling my duties as MPC, I traveled to each of my nine states, visiting and/or calling their respective USTA district offices. I would inquire about the location of minority tennis players, obtain their contact information, and discuss with them their interest in the sport. Then, I would tell them it was incumbent upon them to inform the local USTA district office that they wanted a representative to come and see them in person. From there, someone at the district office would call and invite me to one of their local events, affording me an opportunity to speak with interested players. On some occasions, I would be the keynote speaker at the events, sharing about the USTA's rules and regulations. There were many articles in the local newspapers and advertisements on the local radio stations.

Sometimes, the results of my efforts were favorable. Other times, they were not. Nevertheless, I was determined to keep striving to assist as many players of color as I could in gaining membership to the USTA. Furthermore, I was adamant about learning all I could to be effective in my position. John Sheffield, one of my coworkers, taught me good time management as it relates to travel. He suggested when traveling to a location, it would be best to arrive to the location a few hours early or if the appointment was scheduled first thing in the morning, I should attempt to arrive to the city the night before. Following those guidelines would allow extra time built into the schedule just in case an unexpected occurrence transpired. When it came to eating while in transit, my coworker suggested waiting until we arrived at our location and had scouted out the place; then, we could relax and eat. Using his method, I discovered many benefits therein and adopted the method as my own, learning to travel in the most efficient and timely manner while executing punctuality.

After a year in the position, my results and engagement with the local district offices began to become a bit more fluid. To increase my opportunities to connect with aspiring players, I would host tennis clinics while I was near some of the interested parties, giving me additional opportunities to interact with them, while attending to and addressing their concerns or needs.

Coach Lash, an acquaintance of mine, called one day and said, "Venus and Serena are going to be superstars. They are here in Winston, Salem. Do you want to speak to them?" At that point, the Williams sisters had already become well-known, making a name for themselves as they broke into the realm of tennis, hailing from their hometown of Compton, California.

In 1992-3, I attended the Super Show in Atlanta where superstars from all sports (basketball, football, etc.) attend and participate. It was there that I had an opportunity to meet Richard Williams and his daughters Venus and Serena, who were about 10 and 9 years of age respectfully and in elementary school. From there, we developed a relationship that continues to this day. We still communicate on occasion, and I remain as a confidante to them. As a result of my affiliation with Richard Williams, I was able to attend *one* of the Grand Slams of Tennis: the Wimbledon tournaments in England. I was over the moon with excitement because England is the heart of tennis as that is where tennis has its roots, beginning as lawn tennis on grass courts, where all the players wore white. Also Richard and I share a mutual wonderful and gracious friend Dr. O'Neil Culver (whom I introduced Richard to several years ago).

Later, through other connections I had made throughout my involvement in the tennis profession, I had opportunities to attend two other Grand Slams: once to the French Open in Paris and many times to the U.S. Open in New York. The only Grand Slam I have not yet attended is the Australian Open.

Attending the Grand Slams was an overwhelming experience each time. Being amidst international citizens who spoke a variety of languages and represented cultures different from America was a pleasure as I took in the varied styles of their attire and how they interacted with others around them. Of all that made the people from different lands unique, the one commonality we all held was the excitement and interest in tennis matches, which was demonstrated in our enthusiasm while watching the professionals play. Listening to all the voices around me, I began to think I needed to learn some languages because I intended to continue traveling and being multilingual would allow me to communicate with others.

What a Treat!

In 1996, the Summer Olympics were held in Atlanta, GA, and I had the extreme pleasure of partaking in the festivities as a volunteer organizer in the tennis portion, which was held at Stone Mountain Tennis Center. To ensure the success of the tennis tournaments, all of the organizers were required to meet and discuss what was needed to ensure the tournaments went smoothly. We scheduled players for specific time slots and against particular opponents within the tournaments, promoted the tournaments to the general public, spoke to various groups to solicit their attendance at the Olympics, gained additional volunteers, and verified the professionals had what was required for them to participate effectively.

My role shifted day to day over the two-week period as the need arose. One day, I checked the tickets of the guests;

while on another day, I made sure the crowds were orderly. With the number of people who were in attendance, orderliness was a must. The attendees filled blocks and blocks. I had never seen as many people from so many different countries, speaking a variety of languages, attend a singular event as I saw there at the Summer Olympics. It was the most incredible, spectacular event I have ever attended. My disposition toward being in the midst of it all is almost indescribable. I enjoyed the energy of the Olympics and all of the various portions that comprised the Olympics as a whole, but one of the most memorable portions was the candle lighting ceremony that took place at the beginning. Attending the event was the opportunity of a lifetime, and I still have the shirt and shoes from the uniform I wore during those two weeks.

Although I served as a volunteer, I did receive a 'Thank You' in the form of a trip, which gave the option of going to Hawaii or Colorado. The popular choice for many may have been Hawaii with the palm trees, beaches, and natural pineapples, but I opted for skiing along the snow-filled slopes in Colorado.

After working in the position of MPC for approximately four or five years, I left the position and subsequently left Atlanta. After my time in Atlanta, I took a few classes in South Carolina and allowed my mind and body to receive much-needed rest.

Tragedy and Politics

Then, in August of 2001, I transitioned from the South, where I had spent my life up to that point, and moved to San Francisco. Two weeks later, 9/11 tragically shook the United States, leaving thousands of Americans dead in its wake. On that morning, I went to work to find the doors locked. As I traversed the streets of downtown San Francisco wondering what was the cause of the locked doors of the office building in which I worked and the mostly empty streets, I overheard conversations here and there about the tragedy that had struck our land in New York, impacting Americans from the east coast to the west and from the north to the south.

Little by little, the blanks began to fill in as to why many businesses were closed that day, why terror permeated the lives of those who had heard of the attack on the Twin Towers, and why people were rushing through the streets trying to get home. The fear and sadness everyone was feeling was shared by me. The situation that left so many questions and not enough answers frightened me, and like many others, I began to call family and friends, especially those back home to check on their state of mind and emotional wellbeing. Over the phone, we provided comfort to one another, even while asking questions no one could answer at that point. In my confusion, I really had no one to turn to physically because I did not know many people because I was new to the city and state. However, I did reach out to the few coworkers I had met during my short time there.

Shortly after my arrival to California, I affiliated myself with Third Baptist Church in San Francisco, immersing myself into the culture with the other parishioners. Pastor Amos Brown is the senior pastor, and he truly loves God, His people, His Word, and politics. Dr. Amos Brown is an African American pastor and civil rights activist. He is the president of the San Francisco branch of the NAACP and has been the pastor of the Third Baptist Church of San Francisco since 1976. Brown was one of only eight students who took the only college class ever taught by Dr. Martin Luther King, Jr. He serves on the board of the California Reparations Task Force. (L.A. Sentinel, 2021).

As a parishioner at Third Baptist, I was able to meet and/or work with many influential politicians, such as former President Bill Clinton and former Speaker of the House, Nancy Pelosi. Additionally, I met many civil rights activists also, such as Reverend Jesse Jackson and Reverend Al Sharpton at Third Baptist.

The current United States Vice President, Kamala Harris and the current California Governor, Gavin Newsom were two politicians I met during my tenure at First Baptist and were able to work alongside them as they campaigned. In 2003, I had the opportunity and privilege to meet VP Kamala Harris and serve on her first campaign when she ran for and won the District Attorney seat for San Francisco in 2003.

For Harris' campaign, I would frequent her office, which was located in Bay View Hunter's Point. There, I graciously completed tasks as needed, from making phone calls, opening mail, canvasing streets to put out campaign signs, and going to fundraiser locations to ensure everything was prepared for the impending event. As part of Harris' fundraising team, it was my responsibility to arrive to the event location prior to her arrival, so when she arrived on the scene, she could speak to her constituents without hesitation.

Campaigning took place in a variety of communities, causing me to travel to attend the different events at which she would make an appearance. Prior to her arrival to the location, I would be called by staff members who traveled with her, or I would call them to pinpoint the specific time of her arrival to keep everything running smoothly. Harris spoke at the Department of Education, Office of Civil Rights, as our keynote speaker at a Black History event around 2003-4.

In total, Harris served two terms as District Attorney from 2004-2010 and was the first Black woman to do so. A few people assisted during her first campaign, while many more assisted during the second one. I was able to assist very little on her second campaign because on August 29, 2005, Hurricane Katrina devastated coastal areas of the Gulf Coast states of Alabama, Louisiana, and Mississippi, including the city of New Orleans. It was among the greatest of natural disasters to ever strike the United States (National Weather Service). Understanding the devastation and loss families were suffering as a result of the natural disaster, I elected to volunteer in Biloxi, Mississippi around the latter part of September, through FEMA, to assist those in need, while I was working for the Department of Education.

In 2004, I assisted with Governor Gavin Newsom's campaign during one of his fundraising parties when he was running for mayor of San Francisco. He won the election and remained in office until 2011. On occasion, I hosted several fundraisers for him. Also, he would come to Third Baptist Church, and we hosted an outdoor fair for him where he spoke to his constituents. As with Harris' campaign, I worked with Newsom's staff to prepare for his arrival. Ms. Vera Clanton, a member of Third Baptist who owned apartment buildings in San Francisco, was a big contributor for Newsom. She made sure I was there to run events and host for her.

Frederic J. Brown/AFP/AFP/Getty Images
(cnn.com)

I enjoyed engaging in the political arena and kept my hands to the plow as much as possible. As a matter of fact, I was in attendance at President George Walker Bush's second inauguration party in 2004-5 at the White House. Also, I attended the various balls and parties, mainly in support of Condoleezza Rice, who served as the Secretary of State. I had heard much about her from the time I was a little girl. She had grown up in Birmingham, Alabama. Everyone was very proud of her and in great support of her. She was rumored to be very intellectual and scholastic, causing her to skip grades in her formative education.

A few years later, I moved from the San Francisco area, causing my path with Harris and Newsom to diverge. As a result, I have not had the pleasure of working with them since I left the area. However, my path and Harris' did cross on one occasion when she was running for senator. While attending an event at the University of Southern California, where Harris was the keynote speaker, she spotted me in the crowd and sent London Breed (San Francisco's current mayor) over to speak to me to see how I had been doing and what I had been engaged in. I responded by saying, "I'm here now in L.A."

Education and Equity

While attending Third Baptist Church and assisting on various political campaigns, I was an investigator for the Department of Education for Civil Rights in San Francisco, during the time of the No Child Left Behind Act (NCLBA). I served in that position from approximately 2001-2008. During that time, as a result of writing reports and investigating cases, I honed my writing skills as a I learned to be a journalist, collecting information and subsequently writing reports. All in all, serving as an investigator was very rewarding and a great learning experience. As I traveled and investigated, I came across a variety of cases, where students had allegedly experienced discrimination of many types. Some entered complaints regarding accessibility issues when they were not permitted to enter into mainstream classrooms and were forced to be segregated, while still others had complaints regarding equal opportunity in sports participation.

According to Title IX, The U.S. Department of Education's Office for Civil Rights (OCR) enforces, among other statutes, Title IX of the Education Amendments of

1972. Title IX protects people from discrimination based on sex in education programs or activities that receive federal financial assistance. Title IX states: No person in the United States shall, on the basis of sex, be excluded from participation in, be denied the benefits of, or be subjected to discrimination under any education program or activity receiving Federal financial assistance (U.S. Dept. of Education, 2021). With the support of Title IX, I was able to ensure girls' rights were not violated when they participated in sports. In some instances of promoting equity in sports, the number of men's teams had to be reduced in order to make room for women's teams. Furthermore, when situations warranted it, I would check their equipment to ensure it was not substandard and in working order. Due to my background in sports, my team trusted me to surveys the sports equipment due to my knowledge from my previous experiences in sports.

Billie Jean King, a great tennis champion, was a strong proponent of Title IX, along with Cris Evert, Martina Narvatalova, Katrina Adams (former president of the USTA), and many other tennis players who promoted women in sports.

Living and working in San Francisco taught me a great deal about life and allowed for an abundance of opportunities to work in my church and in the political arena.

A Leap of Faith

At the end of summer 2008, I made a conscious decision to leave my well-paying, comfortable job working for the Federal Government in the Department of Education. My overwhelming desire to follow my passion of teaching tennis was aching within my core, and I was compelled to answer the call. So, I took a leap of faith and submitted my letter of resignation, surrendering my position back to the government, one that had met all my financial needs. With a strong desire to seek employment in the field of tennis, I packed up my office and my home and moved from San Francisco to Los Angeles without a job prospect. The only thing I had was my faith, desire, and belief that everything would go well. The three things I had in my corner were a sufficient amount of savings, my previous experience in tennis, and my belief that God would see me through.

The timing was critical. If I had not done it at that very moment, I would have never made the transition. Was I fearful? Yes! Were my nerves rumbling around in my stomach? Yes! But, I was aware I could not allow fear to grip my heart and render me immobile. II Timothy 1:7 says, *"For God has not given us a spirit of fear, but of power and of love and of a sound mind."* In that moment, I knew I had to stand on the Word of God I had proclaimed for the majority of my life. I could not be swayed by the words of naysayers or those who believed they knew what was best, even when they had my best interest at heart. I had to do what I knew was right for my life. So, without taking a look back, I moved forward and quelled the trepidation that attempted to rise up within me. For, Apostle Paul stated in Philippians 3:13-14, *"Brethren, I count not myself to have apprehended: but this one thing I do, forgetting those things which are behind, and reaching forth unto those things which are before, I press toward the mark for the prize of the high calling of God in Christ Jesus."* So, once I began my transition, I knew I had to stay in the press toward my goal.

Taking the leap of faith was not easy, but it was necessary. If I wanted to turn the corner in my life and follow my passion, I had to make the transition, knowing the Almighty God would be with me the entire time. My very life's existence depended on it. In the midst of a challenging and unsettling situation, I allowed the peace of God which passeth all understanding to be my comfort. I allowed the bosom of the Lord to be my resting place. I took God at His Word that He, and He alone, is my strong tower, and I decided to abide in the shadow of the Almighty, knowing in the end, it would all be well. Afterall, I was marking out my life's journey!

When I began looking for employment in the Fall, I called the La Mirada Tennis Center and was disappointed when they told me they could not hire me at that time. The person to whom I spoke said, "If you had called during summer, I could have hired you." I understood, said good-bye, and disconnected the call. One week later, to my surprise, I received a call from that same center. Someone called to say the head coach was in a coma and asked if I could avail myself for work the next day. I told them unfortunately, I could not get there that soon, as I was not anticipating their call. I offered to be there in two to three days, explaining I needed to plan to travel there. The person readily consented and said, "I'll see you then."

Once I began my employment, I remained at the La Mirada Tennis Center for approximately ten years until I had completely transitioned to the greater Palm Springs area. At one point, prior to my relocation, I was still training clients there while building my clientele in Palm Springs, as the center held my space as long as I paid my monthly fees, which allowed me to have a court available to train clients.

I had been in Los Angeles for a year or two and had heard Karen Bass was seeking election in the state legislature. I believed she would be a good candidate for the local position and decided to work on her campaign during that time around 2010-13. From there, she relocated to D.C. and served a term or two. During that time, she was over the Black Caucus. Presently, she is the mayor of Los Angeles.

Upon residing in the Palm Springs area, I was able to reconnect with Peter Burwash International (PBI). Peter and I had originally met around 2008-10. I have fond memories of him being very welcoming and warm. He had a very kind spirit. We discussed working together; however, it was years before it would manifest. As part of

PBI, Peter developed high caliber tennis programs internationally via many exclusive and elitist hotels, such as the Four Seasons, Marriott, and Ritz Carlton.

Then, in the latter part of 2022, the perfect timing became available via the current director of PBI, Jim Leopold, who had worked with Burwash for years. Unfortunately, I am not working directly with Peter because he passed away last year, earlier in 2022. I will always remember Peter Burwash as a wonderful gentleman who always treated me kindly as I ventured into coaching.

Rick Macci is a great tennis coach whom I learned a great deal about tennis teaching techniques. Also, he served as Venus and Serena's coach during the early years.

John Embree is yet another notable person I came in contact with, as I received my license via his tennis program. Like Peter Burwash, he always presented himself in a helpful manner with a kind demeanor. Embree is the CEO/Executive Director of the USPTA and has a long history in tennis. "He has held a wide variety of influential tennis industry roles for more than 30 years" (United States Professional Tennis Association, 2023).

Watch for the continued growth and success of Alicia Parks and Coco Gauff, both young up and coming professional tennis players.

Much continued success for Bruthas on Tennis who host a wonderful podcast, in which I had an opportunity to participant.

Final Thought

From pickleball's inception in 1965 to approximately 2020, not one professional player or amateur player considered pickleball a threat to the future of the sport of tennis. However, after the COVID-19 pandemic broke out in 2020 and people sought out an activity in which they could engage safely while social distancing and being entertained, Pickleball's popularity increased tremendously. People around the country began engaging in the sport, causing many questions to circulate.

Primarily, the newfound interest caused athletes as well as spectators to question whether or not pickleball's existence and popularity are posing a threat to the game of tennis. As I mentioned in a previous chapter, there is certainly room for more than one sport to pique and hold the interest of players.

Think of it this way: If someone has a love for hamburgers, he/she has an opportunity to dine at McDonald's, Wendy's, In-N-Out, Burger King, or Freddy's, without one or the other going out of business just because that hamburger enthusiast decided to dine somewhere else on a given day. All of the hamburger franchises I mentioned have all excelled and are still going strong despite the existence of the other hamburger restaurants.

The same is true for other sports despite the growing popularity of pickleball. For example, notice how football has not canceled out because basketball fans are high in number or vice versa. Nor has soccer canceled out baseball or vice versa. All of the other sports have thrived due to their popularity because of the interest of a segment of our American, and even international, population.

So, when it comes to pickleball canceling out tennis due to its increased popularity, it is not likely that tennis is going to fade away any time soon or at all. In my humble opinion, both sports will continue to flourish!

References

Al Jazeera. 2022. "Serena Williams Timeline: Highs and Lows of Her Tennis Career." aljazeera.com

BAZAAR. 2021. "Venus and Serena Williams on Their Own Terms." bazaar.com

Biography. 2022. "Venus Williams." biography.com

Biography. 2021. "Arthur Ashe." biography.com

Biography. 2021. "Famous Leaders: Entrepreneurs: Bill Gates." biography.com

The Dink Media Team. 2022. "Bill Gates has been playing pickleball for 50 years." thedinkpickleball.com

Encyclopedia Britannica. 2023. "Biography: Warren Buffet." britannica.com

Ferris State University. 2022. "Denise McNair, Cynthia Wesley, Carole Robertson, and Addie Mae Collins." ferris.edu.

Foundation for Economic Education. 2015. "Althea Gibson: A Winning Attitude." fee.org

Geeter, Darren. 2022. Why pickleball has Tom Brady and LeBron James investing. cnbc.com.

Key. 2018. "Lionel Richie."

King, Martin Luther. 2017. "What is Your Life's Blueprint?" Seattle Times.

L.A. Sentinel. 2021. "Rev. Amos Brown Brings Wisdom Guidance to Cal's Reparations Task Force." lasentinel.net

Mackie, Brandon. 2023. "Pickleball Statistics: The Numbers Behind America's Fastest Growing Sport in 2023." pickleheads.com

National Weather Service. "Hurricane Katrina." weather.gov

Onix. 2023. The History of Pickleball. onixpickleball.com

Primetime Pickleball. 2023. Pickleball is a combination of what 3 sports? primetimepickleball.com.

United States Department of Education. 2021. Title IX and Sex Discrimination.

United States Professional Tennis Association. 2023. "USTPA Administration: John Embree." ustpa.com

USA Pickleball. 2023. "History of the Game." usapickleball.org

Wall Street Journal. 2023. "John McEnroe Is Playing Pickleball for $1 Million? You Cannot Be Serious." wsj.org.

CPSIA information can be obtained
at www.ICGtesting.com
Printed in the USA
JSHW041917260523
42045JS00003B/30